THEIR PLACE IN HISTORY

A time when boys became men, patriotism and the glamour of war turned to fear, loneliness, trench foot, American blood saturated foreign soil, and once handsome young men floated in unheard of seas.

Sharon J. Nicholson

THEIR PLACE
IN HISTORY

Copyright © 2009 by Sharon J. Nicholson.

Cover: WWII PBY in flight off the shores of Whidbey Island.
Title Page: Brenner Pass, Italy
Back Cover: Author's summary insert within a Liberty Ship photo

Library of Congress Control Number: 2009908939
ISBN: Hardcover   978-1-4415-7045-1
               Softcover   978-1-4415-7044-4

All rights reserved. No part of this book may be reproduced or transmitted in any form or by any means, electronic or mechanical, including photocopying, recording, or by any information storage and retrieval system, without permission in writing from the copyright owner.

This book was printed in the United States of America.

To order additional copies of this book, contact:
Xlibris Corporation
1-888-795-4274
www.Xlibris.com
Orders@Xlibris.com

Contents

Forward 11
1933 Nick Carter 13
1938 Thomas Bernard "Bernie" Hingston 25
1940 Glenn H. Lane 31
1940 Milton Henry Littke 47
1941 Harry Hackett Ferrier 57
1941 Harold Johnson 67
1941 Robert "Bob" S. Biddle 79
1942 Lawrence "Doc" Dykers 86
1942 Virginia Madeline Wells 95
1942 Dorothy "Dot" Virginia Sheehan and
       Kenneth Carl "Casey" Baier 101
1942 Ray "John Wayne" Myers 108
1942 Donald Gordon 116
1943 Leon "Lee" Sher 127
1943 Laurin "Bud" Zylstra 133
1943 Wesley "Wes" Rein Zylstra 141
1943 Jim Ronhaar 155
1943 Hank Koetje 187
1943 Adolph Paul "Mickey" Meisch Sr. 226
1943 Robert "Bob" Muzzall 233

Acknowledgements

Special acknowledgements are extended to author Chris Saxman for sharing HANK'S STORY, Margaret Peterson for introductions to her cousins and classmates who left Whidbey Island to serve their country, Helen Chatfield-Weeks, and Trudy Sundberg for their support and encouragement. Most of all, to the veterans for sharing of their stories, their legacies given to me to share with you. I love them all.

Greatful thanks to Jim Ronhaar and Marilyn Pitchford for their multiple readings and editing skills to maintain the integrity of the memories of the these veterans. Pictures have been provided by those interviewed unless otherwise noted.

Proceeds from purchasing THEIR PLACE IN HISTORY will he donated to the Whidbey Island PBY MEMORIAL FOUNDATION.

Preface

Buried within all true stories are pieces of our own history. For generations, oral history has taken us to specific times and places outside our lives and imagination. They are the basis for our culture, customs, music and literacy; all of which makes us human and makes the teller of these true stories eternal. If we're lucky enough to meet others who graciously share their stories, we have found irreplaceable treasures. I have been blessed with family and new friends who have shared their experiences so that I might write them down. Thank God I learned early in life just how important it is to write these stories from their place in history.

I was only eight when John Clinard, my great-grandfather, would tell me true stories about his youth in Missouri during the Civil War. He told me stories of how his family emigrated from Germany, and how he brought his family from Sweetwater, Missouri, to Fort Benton, Montana in an immigrant railroad car. The family occupied the front half with the livestock and farm equipment in the other half. I always got a Baby Ruth candy bar from him for being a good listener. Unfortunately, he took all of his wonderful stories and family legacies with him to the grave. I wish I could trade all those candy bars for one of his true stories in writing.

Johna Christensen, a sorority sister, was only six when the Nazis marched in to Copenhagen, Denmark. She came into our classroom and read chapters of her autobiography to my students. My students had a once-in-a-lifetime experience to ask questions of someone who had lived the history they could only read about. They practiced taking notes; they listened without candy bars for a reward and gave her suggestions for her book. Unfortunately, it was not published before she died.

I shared my uncle's memoirs as a B-24 tail gunner, flying twenty-six missions over Italy, Austria, and Germany, before his plane was shot down over Brenner Pass. He was captured by the Germans, and as a prisoner of war marched to Nuremberg and then another ninety miles in the harshest of weather conditions to Moosburg. As a POW, he was liberated by General Patton's Army. I worked on writing a creative nonfiction manuscript (true story) from his memoirs, wishing he was still here to tell us more about his experiences firsthand. My students took notes and asked questions. More importantly, the memoirs gave them enough curiosity to do their own research on WWII. I also learned from my students' research reports that they shared in class.

Margaret Peterson, another sorority sister, suggested that I interview her cousins that were WWII veterans living in Oak Harbor. This began an explosion of remarkable interviews with WWII veterans from all branches of the military. After a series of interviews, we reviewed their true stories together until they were satisfied with the results. This wonderful generation of great-grandparents allowed me to write down their memories, do my research, and ask halfway-intelligent questions. I love them for it, as do their families. Some veterans trudged through malaria-infested swamps in the Pacific, while others rode the waves and skies in 140 mile per hour williwaws in Alaska. They tossed nightly in bunks and tents, waiting for Japanese kamikazes to attack or the German snipers hidden in caves in the Italian Alps to shoot them in the back.

These are the stories of boys who became old men before reaching the age of twenty-one and worried about their folks back home. They did "their jobs" in the Pacific, Alaska, China, Burma, India, the Panama Canal, France, Italy, Norway, Africa, the Philippines, and in all the other places we've forgotten. Time has been my enemy; *Their Place in History: WWII Anthologies* is an honest glimpse into the realities of war from their perspective and experiences.

Forward

Sharon Nicholson has made a research project of Oak Harbor veterans of WWII a priority in her life for the past two and one-half years. She refers to this project as a blessing to have the opportunity to interview twenty of the most gracious veterans, who opened their hearts and duffel bags of memories to bestow their priceless legacies before they go. Because of the her steadfastness, many of the young heroes she writes about will have lived long enough to know that they gave us one last legacy for their families, students, and friends. *Their Place in History* may be the last chance we have to document their noble deeds. One of the captivating aspects of this anthology is that the stories are told by these veterans in their own words, revealing bravery, courage, and modesty.

These veterans are the same "youngsters" who have survived long enough for us to ask them one more time, "What did you do during the war?" You will get the same modest response: "Just doing my job," which must have been drilled into them during their basic training. Only a few of those youngsters during WWII remain. They are leaving us on a daily basis and taking their stories with them. Sharon plans to make every effort to capture another twenty stories—some are even waiting to tell their stories and work on a second book. This unique and inspiring book will be of interest to many Oak Harbor residents, WWII history students, young and old alike, and Whidbey's military families.

Trudy Sundberg, author, playwright, and journalist

Nick Carter

The Fighting Fanny Bee

In Loving Memory Of...

Lester D. "Nick" Carter

October 19, 1915 ~ November 15, 2007

Husband, Father, Grandfather, Teacher and Friend...

Nick "Lester Duane" Carter was one of four high school graduates who had planned to join the Navy. Nick had grown up in Plains, a small town with a population of nine hundred to one thousand, north of Missoula, Montana. He enlisted in Butte, Montana, on his eighteenth birthday in 1933. At the time it seemed like the logical thing to do. Our country was not at war; it was during the Depression, and jobs were scarce. Nick said, "And I had it planned so I could retire after thirty years at age forty-eight."

"I went by train to Salt Lake City, Utah, where I was actually sworn in to the Navy. From there, eighteen new recruits boarded the train for San Diego, California, for basic training. This was my first time to see the Pacific Ocean. I had plans for entering aviation training; that option was closed as well as my first choice had been to go to music school and play in the Navy band. The music school wasn't taking applicants. So I was advised to go on one of the battleships or one of the two carriers that had a band aboard the ship. So I agreed to go on the *USS Lexington* (CV-2)."

Nick's first sea duty was aboard an old four-stacker, the *USS Twiggs*, number 144, a Wickes-class destroyer left over from WWI. Nick draped his hammock over his sea bag, which held all his earthly possessions and went aboard for his first trial run to Long Beach. His first trial was to remember to duck real low to get his 72-inch-plus frame and the bulky sea bag on his shoulder every time he entered a hatchway. They got over to the *Lexington* from the *Twiggs* motor launch. The carrier was about the biggest thing Nick had ever seen. When it rolled one direction, the gangway went underwater, so you had to wait until it rolled toward the motor launch and cleared the water. Then you jumped off, ran up the gangway, and entered the ship.

Nick was temporarily assigned to the X division. He didn't know one end from the other, and his first routine operation meant a complete sweep down of the ship's deck. The *Lexington* is an aircraft carrier with about two and a half acres of flight deck, and every square inch was swept. His first long-range cruise was along the east and the Panama Canal. Heading back toward the west coast, they stopped in Guantanamo Bay, Cuba, for three weeks for gunnery training with the antiaircraft guns projected five-inch shells.

"I continued my training when the ship was scheduled for short-range target practice in the Pacific. The target plane towed the target about one thousand feet behind on a predetermined, scheduled course. Each gun had colored projectiles to identify successful hits. After the first shot was fired, I experienced for the first time the explosive percussion of the blast, the lost sense of smell, and smoke roiling into my vision. I couldn't see anything but flame, and they did this three times in succession, and the shots were seldom accurate. This was not a pleasant experience for me.

"The Fourth Division also had the motor launch and that looked interesting to me, so I nagged a second-class boatman's mate to join the motor launch crew. In July, I was finally assigned to the motor launch crew. A crew of six to eight aviation people with aircraft parts was aboard the fifty-foot supply boat. My excitement waned as we neared the nine-hundred-foot *Lexington*.

"The coxswain yelled, 'Don't hook up. Follow the ship out to sea and calmer water.'

"The waves only got higher and the troughs deeper while Eddy Yonts and I were bailing water only to have the wind blow it back into the boat. After a half hour of the boat rolling in the waves from bow to stern, everyone aboard was seasick as well. It was hard to bail seawater from the boat and heave from your own stomach at the same time.

"Eight-inch cables with hooks designed were to be attached through a ten-inch ring on each end of the boat. The cables alongside were hooked to the aft, but neither Eddy nor I could get the cable hooked to the bow.

"The coxswain yelled down, 'Hook on, hook on!'

"When the coxswain in the boat pocket ordered the hoist, the aft of the boat was elevated to a seventy-degree angle with the sixteen-ton boat dangling above abnormal storm waves as high as thirty feet. On the second attempt, we got it hooked on properly. That sixteen-ton boat nearly filled with seawater and a sick crew, shuddered as it was hoisted up toward the pocket.

"Just as we reached the starboard boat pocket, the ship listed to the starboard side, and all the seawater from the flight deck ran into our boat. The side legs of the motor launch broke, flipping most of the aviation crew and water into the boat pocket. The motor launch crew was still in the boat, which was now hanging precariously from the boat pocket. The ship's carpenters had to drill holes in the boat and drain the water out until they could elevate it into the boat pocket. This had been, to date, the most frightening experience of my life. I wasn't so sure now that I wanted to be in the motor launch division."

Nick had taken an interest in the aircraft squadron, so he and his buddy Eddy Yonts got transferred to the BT-1 aviation squadron of dive-bombers. Now Nick had his feet on the ground at North Island, but still operated on the *Lexington* for operations. It was during this period in his Navy career that he feels he grew up. In January of 1935,

Nick was transferred to V-2 Division, which takes care of the flight deck of the *Lexington*.

"My first experience in the V-2 Division would have horrendous results that he would always remember. The aircraft were lined up on the flight deck for takeoff, and there was a chock man, 'brown shirts,' on each side to pull out the chocks/wedge as they walked the planes up the flight deck for takeoff. Chocks were placed behind the wheels to keep the plane from rolling back into the plane behind him. They were also placed in front of the wheel as the pilot revved up his plane.

"As the skipper of the squadron rolled up to the takeoff spot, I didn't have the chocks in front of the wheel reversed so they could be pulled out quickly. The skipper had his plane engine revved up to full power for takeoff into twenty-five to thirty knots of wind before the plane could take off, and the pilot released the brake. The 'yellow shirt' was supposed to check the chocks before he signaled all clear to the pilot. He didn't notice that I wasn't able to pull one of his chocks clear of the left wheel. In a matter of a split second, the pilot of the Great Lakes Dive Bomber lifted his foot off the brake. His plane took an immediate nosedive; the prop hit the deck, spun the plane around, chewing up the flight deck. I thought my Navy career had ended right there.

"Everyone involved were called up to the bridge. The captain heard the pilot's story first. Because the flight deck officer should have checked the chocks before giving the all-clear signal to the pilot, I was dismissed. However, it wasn't long after that I was transferred to the VB-1 squadron.

"During 1935, North Island was home to all four of the Navy's carriers—the *USS Langley*, *Lexington*, *Saratoga*, and *Ranger*. During the 1930s, activities at the air station were of fundamental importance to the development of combat tactics and logistical support systems that became the foundation for the subsequent success of the Pacific Theater by Navy carriers in the war against Japan.

"I participated in the search in early July of 1937 ordered by President Roosevelt for aviatrix Amelia Earhart. Her plane went down somewhere in the Pacific. Nine Navy ships and sixty-six aircraft were involved. The most extensive sea and air search took place in naval history when we scoured 250,000 square miles of the Pacific at the cost of $4 million. The United States government reluctantly called off the search after seventeen days of intense attempts to find some trace of Amelia Earhart."

At this point, Nick and Eddy were transferred in August of 1940 to the ORA (Overhaul and Repair Assembly) as aircraft mechanics on North Island. In the beginning, Nick worked in the section for engine assembly. Prior to the war, Navy aircraft was being refurbished, repaired, and overhauled at North Island. In 1941, when Pearl Harbor was attacked, Nick was promoted to Chief while still working on the test line.

The overall structure of the facilities was revised overnight at North Island. Nick was now in charge of the test line, and the crews worked around the clock in three shifts. The personnel worked in one of six sections, rotating with one day off. Planes waiting on the test line to be deemed structurally sound that had numbered two or three now numbered thirty-five. Immediately after Pearl Harbor was bombed, a squadron of Army Air Corps P-38s from March Field arrived and provided an important part of the coastal defense.

Now as Chief Petty Officer Carter, Nick was in charge of the mechanical and ground testing. More experienced personnel were required, and Nick's responsibilities increased from 1942 to September of 1943 on North Island. One of those new responsibilities was a young Treva Schultz, from Iowa. She had come to San Diego to visit with her grandfather and uncle. When she met Nick, from Plains, Montana, she was working in a French dressmaker's shop. They were married October 7, 1942, while Nick was stationed on North Island.

Civilian men and women came to work at North Island to help support the operating forces in the Pacific. Those forces included over a dozen *aircraft carriers*, the *Coast Guard, Army, Marines*, and Seabees. In September of 1943, the Navy chose to give out some commissions to enlisted personnel; Nick and three other men were commissioned as ensigns. He was transferred to the Transitional Land Unit (TLU) near Miramar where the focus had changed from land-based single-engine bombers to land-based four-engine bombers such as the PB4Y-1, built by Consolidated Aircraft in San Diego, California.

In May of 1944, Nick was transferred to a carrier aircraft service unit (CASU-2) in Pearl Harbor, specifically Barbers Point. The new air station quickly became a hub of aviation activity as the Navy amassed forces in Hawaii to carry the war across the Pacific. Base operations centered on working up carrier air groups and squadrons for deployment to combat operations farther west. Again, Ensign Carter was the aircraft maintenance officer at Barbers Point for another four months with the CASU-2 to work on various planes.

The *USS Fanshaw Bay* (CVE-70), an escort (often called jeep) carrier, had returned to Pearl Harbor about June 1, 1944, for replenishment, training, and final preparations for the assault on Saipan. When Nick boarded the escort carrier, he was seriously mistaken as to the duties of that carrier: "I thought they would be ferrying aircraft from the United States to the forward areas. The *Fanshaw Bay* became a part of the Navy Amphibious, also known as the *Fighting Fanny Bee*.

"Our duty became more hazardous when our pilots gave aircraft cover support for the Marines landing on several islands, including Saipan. I was now the aircraft maintenance officer for *all* aircraft operations aboard the *Fanshaw Bay*. That included repairing and/or replacing any damaged or worn-out parts of the planes, the engines, armaments, or equipment.

"On the *Fanshaw Bay*, we carried the Grumman F4F Wildcats and later on the FM-2s, which were stubby naval fighters. They were obsolete against the Japanese Zero. The larger F6Fs (Hellcat) were more heavily armed, built for superior tactics, ruggedness, and firepower made it more than a match for its adversary. The F6F was responsible for more kills than any other fighter plane in it's time. Some Grumman Torpedo Bombers:, TBFs, GMs, and TBMs were also aboard, which was the finest torpedo bomber of the war. They were extremely stable, rugged, and roomy. Pilots and crew found it heavy on the controls but easy to land on the carrier. They were effective when it was necessary to bore in on the enemy ships at water level in Japanese anti-aircraft fire.

"Ensign Carter's responsibility as hangar deck officer for all aircraft was to make sure that *all* aircraft aboard the carrier were fueled and combat ready, with operational guns and ammunition loaded engines in tune and ready to be lifted from the hangar by the fore-and-aft elevator to and from the flight decks. Practically all planes on the *Fanshaw Bay* were catapulted from the shorter flight deck of this smaller jeep carrier.

"June 15, our U.S. forces invaded Saipan with amphibious forces. The *Fanshaw Bay* had been operating about thirty miles east of Saipan, launching antisubmarine patrols, combat air patrols, photoreconnaissance flights, and providing cover from the Japanese-fortified sections for the Marines landing on the beaches of Saipan. During the amphibious invasion, the *Fanshaw Bay* was attacked twice by enemy aircraft and only by skillful maneuvering avoided two fourteen-inch torpedo shells. I stood on the deck mesmerized as I watched an enemy torpedo literally hit our stern and bounce along the starboard side of the ship below my position several times without exploding. To say that it was a miracle that we weren't blown out of the water is an understatement.

"Two days later, during the course of my next real experience of combat, the ship was under fire from nearly seventy Japanese planes. The aft elevator was hit by a bomb that exploded in midair above the hangar deck, killing fourteen and wounding twenty-three crew members. Fire broke out, and the fire main was ruptured, flooding several compartments in the aft elevator. Members of the repair crew dove beneath the waterline to clear handfuls of asbestos from the intake valves of the pumps. Other crewmen bailed water. The blast had shredded a thick braid of intertwined electrical cables, which had begun to burn. Molten chunks of conductive alloy dripped onto a rack of aerial torpedoes stacked on the hangar deck. Only the Lord knows why they didn't explode and sink the ship.

"During the hours it took to control the damage, everyone was doing their jobs just as they were trained. We were fueled by adrenaline, gut instinct, and the necessity to respond immediately. We had little time to guess what could happen from one moment to the next: training and instinct were our only weapons. The ship was taking on water in the bombed aft elevator, and the first assumption was that we were taking in seawater. Ironically, it was the ship's damage control water system that was punctured and the system was afloat in water. Once the valves were turned off, they quit taking on water. With the fire out, the *Fanshaw Bay* left seriously wounded; she listed three degrees to the port side and settled six feet by the stern. Rear Admiral Bogan was transferred to a destroyer before the *Fanshaw Bay* sailed to Pearl Harbor for repairs.

"On the lighter side, while we were in Pearl Harbor, the crew was given permission to go ashore. Out on the ocean, the sailors had been wearing their blues, absolutely no whites. As the sailors in dress whites came up to me, I was the officer of the day, to go ashore by passing my inspection. One particular sailor will always stand out above the rest. I had to refuse him permission to go ashore. Apparently, he had lost his white uniform hat and was wearing blue. I told him that he had to have a white hat, no exceptions. So the sailor took his blue hat off, wadded it up as he turned away. He returned a few minutes later wearing a very wet and freshly spray painted white hat. I gave him permission to go ashore!

"The *Fanshaw Bay* arrived at Manus on August 28, 1944, for training in preparation and operational readiness for the invasion of Morotai, for which she sailed September 10, with Rear Admiral Clifton A. F. 'Ziggy' Sprague as the new division commander. Her planes flew combat air patrol and support missions, and on September 16th provided air cover for one of the pilots, down just a few hundred feet off the enemy-held shore of Wasile Bay. Diving low, they provided protection until two daring motor torpedo boats dashed and snatched him right out from under enemy shore guns.

"The escort carrier replenished at Manus between October 7 and 12 and then put out for the invasion of Leyte on October 20. Through the first four days of combat on land, sea, and in the air, *Fanshaw Bay* operated off Samar, launching combat air patrol, antisubmarine patrols, observation flights, and drops of psychological warfare material. She continued executing raids and strikes in direct support of the troops ashore. There were airmen, sailors, and Marines fueled with pure adrenaline and possessing the overwhelming fear of being at the wrong location at the wrong moment. I experienced a macabre fascination as I watched horrific combat as it appeared in every direction as if it had been filmed in slow motion. Anything could and did happen during these macabre battle surroundings."

"Warned on October 24 that Japanese surface ships were on the move, all her aircraft flew off the deck of the *Fanshaw Bay* early in the morning to attack the enemy. While the escort carriers retired from the threat of the Japanese surface ships, far faster and with far greater firepower. Just six minutes after her planes were ordered away, the ship came under fire from the Japanese cruisers, and although a heavy squall shielded the escort carriers briefly, she soon began receiving hits. She had taken a third hit under fire from two Japanese destroyers and two cruisers, while American destroyers fought to protect their remaining carriers. The escort carrier *USS Gambier Bay* had been sunk after being capsized in the earlier part of the battle.

"Rear Admiral Sprague's greatest achievement came on October 25 when his Task Unit 77.4.3 (Taffy III) consisting of six escort carriers, three destroyers, and four destroyer escorts fought off the vastly superior Japanese Center Force. The Japanese force consisted of four battleships, six heavy cruisers, and eleven destroyers off the island of Samar in the Philippines. Japanese kamikaze (Divine Wind) Special Attack Corps crashed into the *USS St. Lo* (CVE-63), sending her to the bottom.

"The Battle of Leyte Gulf had been a series of battles involving surface gunnery duels, carriers versus carriers. Combat was full-blown air warfare. The use of kamikazes indicated that the Japanese had expended all their conventional weapons: aircraft, battleships, carriers, destroyers, and cruisers. None of these had stopped the tenacious Americans. But we all knew the inevitable advance toward Japanese Home Island would mean tougher resistance by the enemy.

"The *Fanshaw Bay* shaped her course for Manus, unprotected from the kamikaze assaults, and throughout the day landed planes from her sunk or damaged sisters: *St. Lo* and *Kitkun Bay*. During the Battle of Samar phase of the epic Battle of Leyte Gulf, the *Fanshaw Bay* lost eight men. However, the crew won, enduring esteem and a **Presidential Unit Citation** for the distinguished role she played in these offensive actions.

"The *Fanshaw Bay* replenished at Manus, in the Solomon Islands, from November 1 through 7. Then we returned by way of Pearl Harbor with four additional aircraft with crews that were able to land aboard from other carriers that had been sunk. The *Fanshaw Bay* could take on emergency landings, but aircraft were unable to take off. The damage sustained to the essential catapult track for aircraft launching required that they return to San Diego for battle damage repairs. I spent the remainder of 1944 in San Diego.

"This was perhaps the first occasion since June of 1944 that I could sleep nights without wondering if our crew would live through the night. Treva had been waiting, working and writing to me from her San Diego apartment. Our censored mail had been sporadic. It had been transferred from ship to ship until the right mailbag caught up to the ships. Now that I was stationed in San Diego, I could carry out a daily routine for a normal liberty. This required returning to the base and aboard the *Fanshaw Bay* each night. Treva and I yearned for a routine lifestyle more typical of newlyweds. Sometimes I felt ashamed for being so thoughtless for the young wives and families that would never see their husbands and fathers again."

After a refresher training and patrol duty in Hawaiian waters, the *Fanshaw Bay* arrived at Ulithi on March 14, *1945*, now under the command of Rear Admiral Sprague, commander of Carrier Division 26. The *Fanshaw Bay* resumed its role as the flagship for the invasion of Okinawa on March 21. Four days later, her planes began their preinvasion attacks on the island. For his bravery in combat, Nick was awarded the Bronze Star Medal with Combat V. The aircraft from the *Fanshaw Bay* flew cover for the landings on April 1 and continued daily operations in support of the advance of troops on the island until May 28 when she arrived at San Pedro Bay to replenish supplies. Day after day in April and May, kamikazes attacked American ships, and the *Fanshaw Bay* was not immune. The stress of combat became routine, and that was dangerous because it was easier to make a fatal mistake. During the campaign, the U.S. fleet had stayed offshore to resupply their forces inland and bombard Japanese positions. Eight hundred kamikaze planes were sent to bomb our ships. They sank 32 U.S. ships and damaged 368. Now the U.S. fleet faced the invasion of Japan.

Between June 9 and 27, the *Fanshaw Bay* sailed off the Sakishima Gunto, between Okinawa and Taiwan, to launch air strikes, then provided air cover for minesweeping in the East China Sea through July. Nick performed his duties as before as the ship's aircraft maintenance officer. After calling at Guam and Eniwetok to load aircraft and replenish equipment, *Fanshaw Bay* sailed directly north from Eniwetok to Adak, Alaska.

On August 31, 1945, the *Fanshaw Bay* became the first aircraft carrier to drop anchor in the Japanese homeland waters. The Japanese officially signed surrender papers on the *USS Missouri* on September 2. On September 10, former aircraft commander of the *Gambier Bay* (a composite of thirty fighters and dive-bomber planes) had been reassigned to the *Fanshaw Bay*. Rear Admiral E. W. Litch had the honor of delivering the surrender papers to the Japanese Northern Army for signature. The *Fanshaw Bay* took part in the occupation of northern Japan until returning to Pearl Harbor September 24, 1945.

Most of the Navy's aviation and nonessential personnel were transferred off the *Fanshaw Bay* to other duties as the escort carriers were turned into troop transport carriers from the Pacific home to San Francisco. She arrived on the west coast with Marine Corps passengers November 3. After a return voyage to Tokyo Bay, men of all military services came home to San Diego. Then the *Fanshaw Bay* was placed out of commission in reserve at Tacoma, Washington, August 14, 1946, and sold in September of 1959. Treva Carter was reunited with her personal war hero, Lt. J.g. Nick "Lester Duane" Carter, in San Diego.

USS *Fanshaw Bay* (CVE-70)

After Nick's death, Treva shares her feelings. "During the war, I had been working as a secretary in a medical office within walking distance of their apartment. In 1950, with Christine Louise and James Kane in tow, we accompanied Nick on his new assignment to the Marshall Islands."

Treva said, "I have no regrets, I loved being a Navy wife and the moving from one duty station to another. And we recently celebrated our sixty-fifth wedding anniversary."

The eighteen-year-old boy from Plains, Montana, started his Navy career sporting an enlisted sailor's "white hat." At age forty-eight, Commander Nick Carter retired from the Navy on November 30, 1963, while stationed at NAS Whidbey Island. Like many of our courageous young men and women, Nick said, "I literally grew up in the military. I was proud to serve in the U.S. Navy."

Like other true American heroes, Nick overcame his fears, accepted discipline, developed self-respect and self-confidence.

Thomas Bernard "Bernie" Hingston

Patriotism Was a Family Tradition

It has been my experience as I talk with WWII veterans, including my own father; most of them remain reluctant to share their experiences. As my father put it, "It was my job." Not all of our veterans participated in combat and feel that their experiences were neither adventurous nor heroic. But the fact remains, there are only about 5 percent of our WWII veterans still here to give us one last gift—their memories and firsthand information about leaving their families on Whidbey Island to serve our country.

Bernie Hingston's parents came to live on Whidbey Island in the early 1900s. His ancestral English grandfathers exemplified patriotism for two countries: Canada and America. This family tradition may be traced as far back as the War of 1812. He was born June 13, 1917, in Langley, Washington. Bernie enlisted in the Royal Canadian Air Force before the Japanese bombed Pearl Harbor. He was one of approximately twenty-two thousand Americans who chose to enlist in the Canadian Military to support the British, which had been at war with Germany since 1939.

Bernie is proud of his son M.Sgt. Dennis Hingston. He served as a crew chief and gunner of a rescue helicopter pilot for two tours of duty in Vietnam. Currently his grandson Daniel Hingston, like his father Dennis, is a master sergeant crew chief and the gunner of a rescue helicopter pilot in Iraq. Grandson Daniel has two small children waiting for their dad to come home in September. Bernie must be reliving some of the same fears that his own parents felt for him while he flew his P-40 along the northwest coastline from Alaska to the Puget Sound in search of Japanese intruders.

After graduating from Oak Harbor High School, Bernie spent one year at Washington State University and summers working on the Yukon River. In search of adventure during the summers of 1936-1940, he worked as a deckhand on a stern-wheeler on a run between Dawson and Nenana. His brother Ken and some of his friends had started the tradition ten years earlier by going to Alaska. Jobs weren't that easy to come by during the Depression, so many of them headed north to Alaska via Seattle. The boys from Whidbey had a reputation as hard workers and found it relatively easy to get a job during hard times. Most of them worked the White Pass and Yukon Route on the Canadian National White Star Steamship Company.

Each fall Bernie worked in Seattle as a shipping clerk, spending his paycheck on food and flying lessons. He flew a Piper Cub or the Aeronca, accumulating about fifty hours of civilian flying time. Without a college degree, this experience wasn't enough for the U.S. Army Air Corps. He was finally accepted as the pilot he had always dreamed of becoming by enlisting in the Royal Canadian Air Force.

Bernie was stationed at least once at almost every base on the western Canadian coast. Although he was serving in a combat zone, Bernie was clearly disappointed that he never got to push the button that would fire two, four, or all six of the .50-caliber guns, rapid-fire machine guns, mounted on the wings on his P-40. The Canadian Kitty Hawk, a version of the American Flying Tiger, was built by the Curtis Aeroplane and Motor Company. These fighter planes had one pilot as a crew with six guns that were fixed to fire straight ahead by using a sight that was set on the nose of the plane.

Bernie had a knack for demonstrating his skill as a pilot by flying under the Deception Pass Bridge. Of course, this side trip was not in his flight plans, but it was documented by those on Whidbey Island. Particularly at night, all planes flying within range of Whidbey Island the Deception Pass Bridge were documented as to type of plane, number, and in this case, pilot. Islanders were always thrilled to see one of these "sons" flying the coastlines of Canada, San Juan Islands, and Washington State searching for enemy submarines. But Bernie just wasn't satisfied with his routine role in the Royal Canadian Air Force. The fact was Bernie was bored just flying that P-40 and wanted to see some action. After all, this plane was designed as a fighter plane.

Bernie was well aware that the Japanese occupied at least two of the Aleutian Islands, and these defensive fighter pilots were waiting to bag an enemy. These planes were designed specifically for combat; unfortunately, Bernie and his buddy "Dutch," Thomas Kinsler, from Georgia, were truly disappointed that they never got to shoot their weapons. They considered "getting lost" near Fairbanks, where the P-39s had been transported out of New York via Great Falls, Montana, and picked up by the Russians to fly to the Soviet Union. They had planned to follow the Russians across the Pacific, but they knew their smaller planes couldn't carry enough fuel to make it there and back.

Fortunately, their better judgment probably saved their lives. After all, the Russians didn't let Americans into their country, so only their imagination could foretell the possibilities. If they had added exterior fuel tanks, they might have made the trip. Yet if they were captured by the Russians or shot down, or survived this escapade and made it back, they would be "toast" by the Russians, or the Canadian Air Force upon return. Until Hitler actually ordered the German invasion of Russia, the most disturbing controversial concern facing the Allied forces was whether or not the Russians would join Germany against the Allied forces. The Russians were lend-leasing aircraft from the United States on the pretense of supporting our cause.

Being trained to fly the Mosquito Night Intruder was the personal highlight of his military experience as a pilot. The plane was designed to fly as low as two hundred feet above ground, below enemy guns and searchlights. It was capable of a variety of roles: bombing, path finding, and unarmed photo-reconnaissance flying.

Both Bernie and Dutch had requested a change in orders to go to Europe so that they might transfer back into the U.S. Army Air Corps, but Montreal had put a moratorium on Americans by requiring them to renounce their U.S. citizenship. Neither Dutch nor Bernie were willing to do so; however, they both could be transferred. Dutch arrived in Europe in time to be a part of the air defense on D-day. His plane was shot down, and he was killed.

While waiting in Montreal for his orders to be sent to Europe, Bernie met his future bride. Sgt. Betty Dennis had enlisted in the Canadian Air Force and was stationed and worked in Montreal. Bernie proudly wore his Canadian Air Force wings on his right shoulder and the U.S. Army Air Corps patch on his left. But their courtship would become long distance. Although he missed Betty, he was anxious to follow his buddy in the skies over Europe. But it was not to be.

Bernie was assigned to temporary duty for six months as a ferry pilot, delivering B-17 planes built in Long Beach, California, to Lincoln, Nebraska. There the Army Air Corps had formed their crews, received their orders, and waited for the ferry pilots to deliver the new planes headed for Europe.

In June of 1944, Bernie was sent to India and assigned to the Air Troop Carriers (ATC). Only ten days prior to leaving for India, Betty and Bernie were married. There he flew the Hump Express, known as the CBI (China-Burma-India) run. His C-46 was capable of flying in the high altitudes over the Himalayan Mountains. The pilots required oxygen masks, a radio compass; it came down to experience and instinct. Day and night, in sunshine or monsoon rains, his C-46 hauled fifty-five-gallon barrels of high-octane gasoline, grenades, mortar shells, and general cargo to the struggling armies of Generalissimo Chiang Kai-shek in China. Bernie also transported Chinese troops between bases Chengdu and Kunming in China.

"Twice I had to carry Chinese troops, artillery, aircraft fuel, and twenty-four small horses. The belly of the C-46 was filled with airsick and frightened horses and Chinese troopers. It was the most horrible stinking mess I'd ever smelled. I never forgot those two missions. I made these missions for fifteen months. I had no idea what happened to the supplies once they were unloaded at the bases in China. That aspect of the operation was not all clear. Chaing Kai-shek was at the head of government, but the Maoist forces already had a strong foothold in the interior of China."

Younger and less-experienced pilots flew the planes at their utmost altitude, experienced mechanical failures, storms, and navigational errors, which claimed the crews and troops on nearly four hundred planes. The hump route was often referred to as "Aluminum Alley" by pilots. Except for the radio compass, it came down to experience and instinct. Once some routes were established, the air activity took on the movement and frenzy of a column of ants.

The name Aluminum Alley was appropriate because of the tonnage of aircraft strewn along the ridges of the Himalayan Mountains. The casualty list of pilots and supplies was beyond comprehension; however, it did prove the feasibility of hauling cargo by air. The jungle has long since reclaimed the wreckages. The whole story of the CBI Theater of the war has been relegated to dust-bound books and the memories of those men still with us who flew the hump.

By early 1945, the monthly cargo delivered to China reached forty-four thousand tons, peaking at seventy-one thousand in July. When the war in the Pacific ended in August 14, 1945, it took three months to cut the red tape so Bernie could join his bride. Bernie had enough points to his credit to be the third person to fly from Calcutta, India, home to Fort Dix, New Jersey.

He had to be hospitalized so that he could get his weight up to 175 pounds from 128 pounds. He had been suffering from malnutrition and an extreme case of "jungle rot." He was discharged from Fort Dix; Bernie and Betty joined forces for fifty-seven years.

When I asked Bernie if he had any regrets, thinking he might say something about having wanted to be a fighter pilot fighting Germans, he replied, without further provocation, "I never got to shoot my guns."

Bernie passed away August 14, 2008, here in Oak Harbor. He left his mark as a sailor, Royal Canadian Air Force pilot, U.S. Army Air Corp pilot, active member of the Lions Club, and avid poker player.

Sailor
Royal Canadian Air Force Pilot
U S Army-Air force Pilot
Husband   Father   Grandfather
Firefighter   Lion   Realtor

In Memory Of...

Thomas B. "Bernie" Hingston

1917 ~ 2008

Glenn H. Lane

Down Memory Lane

Pearl Harbor Survivor: *USS Arizona,*
USS Nevada, USS Yorktown

In October 1940, Glenn Lane completed Aviation Radio School and was assigned to Observation Squadron 1 (VO-1) aboard the *USS Arizona* (BB-39). He was advanced to radioman 3/C (qualified in aircraft) in August of 1941. He flew as a radioman/observation/rear gunner from the *Arizona* until December 5. On the morning of December 7, when Pearl Harbor was attacked by the Japanese aircraft carrier, he was aboard the *Arizona.*

"It had been the routine for half of our Navy's warships harbored at Pearl to scour the Pacific Ocean for enemy ships and subs. The Navy ships had identified several Japanese subs in the area, but none took aggressive action. Neither did they identify themselves according to international code. Our naval ships had no authority to attack any of Japan's submarines.

These pictures provided by Glenn, show Glenn wing walking on a choppy sea while being supported by the pilot. He had to attach the line onto the airplane crane in order to elevate the plane to the ship's deck.

One of the *Arizona*'s Vought OS2U Kingfisher planes maneuvers alongside the ship and then hooks on the airplane crane. The pilot for this maneuver on 6 September 1941 is Ensign Laurence A. Williams, and the rear-seat man is Radioman Third Class Glenn H. Lane. Williams was killed on 7 December. Lane survived (National Archives, 80-G-66108 and 80-G-66109).

"Meanwhile, the Japanese fleet was coming across the North Pacific to attack Pearl Harbor. Usually the other half of the fleet would be seen by the aerial surveillance leaving the harbor. There was some concern that they might be attacked in the open sea, and/or the fleet would be considered an act of aggression. The expectation had been that "if" there were to be an attack, it would be shelling at night by the submarines. The 'powers that be' never thought it would be an attack by aircraft, even though someone had devised a theoretical battle or war game in which Pearl Harbor would be attacked by enemy aircraft."

Glenn had asked Lieutenant Junior Grade Mini why the others weren't leaving the harbor. Apparently, the "powers that be" decided that taking the more assertive action may have a negative effect on the negotiations between Japan and the United States back in Washington D.C. The *Arizona* was one of the ships that had just returned to Pearl on December 5, and the other half of them that would be going out on surveillance duty remained in the harbor as well. The Japanese strategy capitalized on the exact day in which all of the battleships would be in the harbor to make the exchange of observation duty. The *Arizona* was due for a major overhaul back in the States and scheduled to leave Pearl Harbor on the thirteenth of December.

"On December 6, a normal Saturday routine, we had inspection and then liberty for the crew. Three of us were on Cinderella liberty, which meant we had to be back at the ship by 1:00 a.m. We had bought some Christmas cards and done nothing else special, but there was a long line at the bus back to the ship. They chopped the line off because the bus was full. The three of us had to take a taxi back into the Navy yard just as the last liberty boat pulled away. We yelled at them to come back, but they didn't. The shore patrol came along and said there were no problems, that we could ride back to the *Arizona* with them. But when we walked up the gangplank, the young ensign on duty was standing right there.

"We saluted and stood there like dummies while he took the report from the shore patrol. Then Smitty, a patrolman, waved good-bye, a signal for me to leave. We went down to our bunks, got our clothes off, and shoved them into our lockers. We turned our butts to the outboard side as if we were asleep. Sure enough, the ensign came down to our division with a couple shore patrolmen. They checked all the empty bunks and wrote down the numbers of the bunks. Some of the guys would stay ashore with their girlfriends. Two seamen and one second class would have been on report that Sunday. Ironically, those who stayed ashore survived the battle and the sinking of the *Arizona* because they were on the beach. If they had been aboard the ship, it was a good chance they would have been killed."

Glenn talked to the guys, and they felt pretty fortunate. Naval Intelligence interviewed Glenn with regard to the integrity of the men who happened to stay ashore the night before the attack. When asked about the Japanese girlfriend of one of the guys, "I told them I hadn't been fortunate to have a girlfriend on the beach with all the Army, Navy, and Marines stationed in Hawaii. You were lucky if you had a girlfriend on the beach. Besides, I had a girl back home." The matter was apparently dismissed.

"Not in the history books was a strategy called 'Operation Orange,' devised by the Navy to send fleets to sortie the Pacific to defend the South Pacific Islands—that is the Philippines, the Marshals, Formosa, or Singapore—'if' they were to be attacked. But the Japanese had at least eight or ten carriers and four or five more first-line carriers, and the United States had two carriers. If we had been out there, the Japanese fleet would have sunk us and there wouldn't have been anyone to pick us up.

"Our anti-aircraft guns on the *Arizona* were next to useless—it stunk! For example, they practiced with a towed target, and the anti-aircraft guns came closer to hitting their plane than the target. I made the mistake of radioing back to the ship that the sleeve was the target, not the plane. My pilot said that he didn't mean for me to radio that to the ship. Be prepared for problems when we got back aboard. After two more target runs, the sleeve had no visible signs of ever being hit. That's how useless our five-inch .25-caliber anti-aircraft guns were. The other guns on the *Arizona* were designed for surface warfare. They were inadequate anti-aircraft guns. The ship was inadequately armed for a war that would be fought in the air. We were not prepared!

"I had a towel loosely knotted around my neck when I was headed for the showers. I heard the sounds of explosions at Naval Air Station on Ford Island. I went topside on the forecastle to investigate.

The Day of Infamy
U.S.S. Arizona
December 7, 1941

"Ford Island was ablaze as I watched another Japanese torpedo plane approaching from the east. It dropped a torpedo aimed at the *USS Oklahoma*. I shouted a warning to the lookouts on the signal bridge before I went below to warn my shipmates that we were under attack. Working my way aft to the aviation workshop, I wanted to wake up any shipmate that was still asleep. General quarters (all hands man your battle stations, this is no drill) was sounded, and I went to my battle station to fight a fire on the quarterdeck. There wasn't any water pressure from the fire hose, and my efforts to put out the fire were useless."

Glenn compares the reality of having been there to the movie *Pearl Harbor* and found many discrepancies from the "dress white," which weren't white but blue. "In the movie everyone had dog tags hanging around their necks. Our servicemen never had any form of identification on their person until February of 1942. Liberty cards were used when they went ashore and returned in a box when they came back aboard their ships.

"The movie shows the Japanese flying into buildings and numerous suicide missions by the Japanese. I clearly recall the Japanese never flew into buildings to blow them up. The Japanese pilots swooped down over the base and dropped their torpedoes and bombs on the ships. The U.S. planes were tied up in tidy rows, which were readily strafed by Japanese Zeroes. They shot down all of our Navy's aircraft from taking off except for two planes that managed to take off. Two young lieutenants, Welsh and Taylor in the Army Air Corps, took to the air in their fighter planes and shot down four Jap planes. Within minutes, Japanese torpedo planes and level bombers began their run on the battleships. Torpedo tracks led to the *USS West Virginia* and the *Oklahoma*."

Glenn, a young farm boy from Iowa and Minnesota, was witnessing history. Born January 29, 1918, he lived on a farm without cash income during the Great Depression. During this time in our history, doctor bills were often paid with a quarter of a butchered beef. It was a time in our history when families like the Lanes shared any abundance of crops with their less-fortunate neighbors, time when the only cash the family had came from selling cream they skimmed from the milk.

"After spending two years working in the Civilian Conservation Corps (CCC) in Minnesota, I worked my way up to a leadership position, which entitled me to $45 a month instead of $30. I drove a Model A Ford with three friends out from Minnesota, through South Dakota, Montana, and Idaho. We found limited work on the reclamation dam at Fort Peck, northwest of Billings on the Missouri River in Montana. I worked on several jobs harvesting crops but came to Washington when we heard there was work on the construction of the Grand Coulee Dam. We worked here in Washington State during late July through September until winter. I usually handled the jackhammer, and Chink was another equipment manager at $.75 an hour, which was the top wage. The others were labors and earned a mere $.40 per hour.

"On our way back home to the Midwest, we camped and cooked our own food. We found a job searching for the common barberry that grew wild near Idaho Falls. The common barberry bush was the host plant for blister rust fungus, infecting the farmers' wheat crops, and they wanted it eradicated. We had to catch the truck early in the morning, and then we were given a shovel, a gunnysack, a bag lunch, and a canteen of water. We were dropped off in the hills and picked up about four in the afternoon. As for snakes, the rattlers didn't bother us if we beat the bushes before we dug them up.

"Ironically, we noticed an old woman in the town of Idaho Falls who had been duped into planting a whole hedge of common barberry bushes around her yard. So we showed her the pictures of the notorious common bayberry and made a deal with her to remove the offending hedge and replace it with the acceptable Japanese bayberry variety for free. We were able to collect our pay from the government for removing her nasty plants and throwing them into our bags. I remember she cooked us a nice chicken dinner too. It was a great deal for both the woman with the illegal hedge and for us. I was grateful to have enough wages to be able to return to Minnesota to help my dad on the farm."

In the spring of 1938, Glenn went back to work for the CCC so that he could send cash income back home to help his dad keep the family farm during those times of great economic depression. His folks saved the money Glenn sent home for him.

"I am proud of the 'work ethic' that was instilled in me by having been raised on a farm, contrary to the city kids who came to the CCC camps not knowing a thing. They didn't even know how to use a shovel or an axe. We had to teach them how to work. I was made crew leader, and the camp was run in military fashion.

"Once WWII had started in Europe, our country would soon be dragged into the war as they had been in WWI. My uncle had been a Marine in WWI, and his advice was to stay out of the Army or the Marines. Because they lived like rats in trenches, one meal a day if they were lucky and they slept propped up in the hole. And they lived in the same clothes for weeks!

"Based solely on the advice of my uncle, I enlisted in the Navy. From there, I was sent to the Great Lakes Naval Training Station situated on the banks of Lake Michigan, the coldest place on this earth. We farm boys were used to wearing the long winter underwear, but on May 1, we were ordered to wear our summer uniforms at graduation. I nearly froze to death in just shorts and a Skivvies shirt.

"I had some military-like experience in the CCC camps, and I knew basic camp decorum. I kept my uniform clean and neat. They made me a color-bearer in which I carried a rifle alongside the flag. We also raised and lowered the flag. I didn't drill with the other recruits, but I had to take the same required exams in which I excelled with high marks. I was voted honor man of my company.

"I had wanted to fly because that meant a few extra dollars each month, but aviation school was full. So they suggested that I get into Aviation Radio School. That too was a choice opportunity for those who wanted to fly. The school took only twenty-five guys every three months for training. I had to wait three months to get into the school in San Diego. I graduated from Aviation Radio School in October 1940.

"Then I was assigned to Observation Squadron 1 (VO-1) aboard the *USS Arizona* (BB-39). I was made seaman first class ($54 a month) within that first year, and I flew in observation planes (OS2U-1). By August of 1941, using extra time to study, I was made third class radioman and also QA (qualified in aircraft). Then a tap on the shoulder by the senior aviator Lt. J.g. James Mini moved me up to the third class radioman from second class until the war started. Ironically, Lieutenant Junior Grade Mini was the son-in-law of Captain Buckmaster, skipper of the *USS Yorktown*, who would become a part of my naval experience in the future."

Glenn was the middle child of three sisters and three brothers. His younger brother Forrest entered the Navy a couple days before the attack on Pearl Harbor. His older brother was drafted into the Army near the end of the war. As railroad engineer, he was stationed in the Philippines in 1945 for two years. Fortunately, neither brother saw combat the same way Glenn had. Most of the crews of the ships anchored at Pearl were up and dressed, had eaten breakfast, not at all as it had been portrayed in the book *At Dawn We Slept*. They had church services right on the ships, and most of sailors were expected to be there or out of sight. Glenn and his buddies had decided they would stay below deck and address Christmas cards that they had purchased onshore.

Pearl Harbor Memories

Glenn said, "I felt like I needed a shower first. So I threw my towel around my neck and picked up my toiletries when we started hearing explosions close to eight. My first thought was that someone had accidentally set off one of the bombs over where the PBYs were located. We climbed up on the deck to see the sailors up on the bridge, leaning on the railing and watching the so-called air show—the bombing over on Ford Island. The brilliant morning sun made it impossible for the sailors to see the Japanese torpedo planes. The officer of the day was down having his breakfast and wasn't there to see what was going on.

"Then I looked down the harbor and saw more planes coming, and I said, 'Uh-oh.' Here comes the Army mock attack on the Navy, and they're doing it on Sunday. Then I saw that the airplane had a torpedo hanging under it. I said to the two kids that were with me, 'That plane has a fish on it. The Army doesn't have any torpedo planes.' Then we saw him drop it near the *USS Oklahoma*. As the plane turned, I saw a great big ol' meatball (rising sun) on the side of the plane. I said, 'Good God, they're Japs.' Then it came down, strafed the side of our ship. We ducked down beside the turret, and it missed us by three or four feet.

"I yelled up to the bridge at those sailors to 'sound the air raid, the Japs are hitting us.' So they started scurrying around up there, and I went down to warn our people on the next deck below. They thought it was some kind of April Fools' joke and told me to 'get out of here.' They didn't believe me or the other two with me. So we went aft where some second and first classes had their bunks. I yelled at them, and they said the same thing. 'You and your April Fools' jokes, you're going to get in real trouble someday.'

"I told them it's an air attack, and just then, a dive-bomber came down, and a bomb hit our ship. It glanced off the turret number 4 and hit the officers' quarters. Three of us immediately headed for our battle stations when we ran into a marine lieutenant, who ordered us to go below and said he'd have no panic aboard his ship. I went on to my battle station that was to fight fires and/or repair the eighth aft deck. Five of us went back to fight the fires (all members of the aviation group manned their battle stations). I don't know where the other two kids went, but they're not alive today.

"Through the billow of black smoke from the torpedoes and bombs, I noticed an officer's hat lying on the deck. I located an uncovered hatch. Inside the depths of the hole was the semiconscious officer. I climbed down holding on the ankle of another sailor and, after the second try, retrieved the same officer by the cuff of his shirt. After asking us what we were doing back there, he gave us an order to man the fire hoses. He would later take the credit for taking command of having ordered the men to man the same trickling fire hoses.

[When Glenn wrote up his account for the military records, he was ordered to change his account of this incident to match the lieutenant commander's statement that he had rescued. The lieutenant commander hadn't remembered being pulled up out of the hold after he was blown into it by the initial bombing and puking up his breakfast on the deck. For his bravery, he received the Medal of Honor, giving no credit to Glenn or the other first-class men who saved the lieutenant commander's life while already manning their battle stations. They had been recommended for the Navy Cross. Glenn had refused to rewrite his statement to dovetail with the lieutenant commander's statement. The first-class men rewrote his and received the Navy Cross, but Glenn did not.]

"Moments later, the *Arizona* was hit amid ship and forward by several bombs piercing the deck, setting it afire. A doctor aboard the *USS Solace*, a hospital ship, happened to have his camera pointed at the *Arizona* during the attack when the forward magazines exploded, setting off millions of pounds of gunpowder, blowing several men off the ship into the oil-slick waters. I was one of those literally blown off the deck of the *Arizona* by a big fireball 'coming through the gates of hell' into shockingly cold and salty water and fighting his way to the surface.

"I swam in two to three inches of oil-covered water to a whaling boat moored near the *USS Nevada* and boarded her as she was getting underway. Some sailors were drowned in the oily water. A strong swimmer, I swam through the oil slick. Once aboard the *Nevada*, I helped another seaman maneuver a five-inch secondary gun until the ship was hit and the gun put out of commission. Once the *Nevada* was the specific target of bombs and torpedoes, I sought shelter in a compartment. Filthy and in shock, I had no interest as to what I might look like. I pounded on the door of the compartment. They mistook me for a mess attendant because of my coal black complexion, oil-covered body, and singed-blacken hair, and I was refused admittance.

"On the first attempt to gain entry, I got a similar reaction from the *Nevada* seamen in the second compartment. The sailor had misrecognized me as a mess attendant or an officer's steward until I removed the shower towel that was still tied around my neck.

"Once I was in the second compartment, another bomb hit the ship directly through the bulkhead and the first compartment, the number 1 case-mate, and killed everyone in there. I had no trouble seeing the gaping destruction because the bulkhead between the two compartments had been annihilated. If they had let me in there, I would have been dead. I helped some other guys get the wounded off the *Nevada* and into boats until I was completely exhausted, and any adrenaline I had left was spent.

"Tugs were pushing the sinking *Nevada* out of the channel going into Pearl Harbor. I was now aware of two monumental factors: (1) I had been severely burned during the explosion on the *Arizona* and 2) the fact that I was blown into the water, the burns on both arms were charred and black. When I started to wash my arms, the skin started to come off with the oily soot. So I left the black oil on my arms. Others had been less fortunate. They were burned raw—their skin pink and puffy. When the corpsman came and noticed that I was bleeding, he gave me a shot of morphine, and it felt like someone had put a nice warm blanket over me."

Glenn was taken to the hospital ship, the *Solace*, by stretcher for treatment for burns and his shrapnel wounds. "The doctor told me that I was a lucky young man. If I hadn't hit the water after the fireball hit when I did, I would have been cooked.

The wards and the hallways were crowded with beds and gurneys filled with burn victims. Still wearing the same remnants of his uniform that Glenn had on during the attack, they peeled all the charred skin off during the second day in the hospital. "I was a beautiful baby pink underneath the burns. I still have scarred places on my hands that never really healed. They never will.

"I was in the hospital ship for thirteen days, and this is the joke. I'm going back to duty, so they gave me a pair of white pants, two sets of Skivvies, two pairs of black socks, no hat, and no shoes. All they had in the storehouse were sizes thirteen, fourteen, and sixes—none of which would fit me. I couldn't go back to duty without shoes, so I was told to go through a pile of soaked, oily, and dirty shoes and look until I found a pair that fit me.

"I took a pair of Skivvies and socks. And whom should I run into? But both the yeomen from the aviation unit that was back there fighting fire with me aboard the *Arizona* and the lieutenant commander that I had dragged out of the hold. He's in his dress whites and gold braid. He said, 'We had heard that you were wounded.'

"I still had the bandages on my wrists from the shrapnel, and I said, 'If you want me to, I'll drop my drawers and I'll show you some more places where they dug out shrapnel.' There was no response. He walked away.

"Then I got orders to go over to Ford Island and report to the newly decorated Lieutenant Mini. I caught the ferry to Ford Island

and rode in a truck to the hangar where everyone was shocked to see me. Lieutenant Mini met me with a hug rather than a salute. 'Boy, am I glad to see you. I didn't think that you were going to make it.' Actually, what happened is Lieutenant Mini had gone to the hospital ship to see me on the fourth day of my admittance, but I was in the shower. I had been standing in the shower, letting the hot water just run over me until I felt clean. When I got out of the shower, I had no towel with which to dry off. I sat down on a bench until corpsmen came by. They had removed the filthy, oily mattress and placed another burn victim in my bed with my chart on it.

"The corpsman made all sorts of threats to write me up for being up out of bed. I still didn't have a towel, but I stood up and told him to get out before I laid him out. Around the corner came a first-class men to see what the entire ruckus was about, and then he told the corpsman to get out. When I asked the first-class men what was wrong with him [the corpsman], he said, 'Feathers,' which was a term meaning he was reserve personnel. So he got me a pair of pajamas and another bunk."

Ironically, Lieutenant Mini had been by to see Glenn when he saw Stanley Lightfoot off the *Arizona* and was badly burnt and beat-up in the bunk with Glenn's name card on it. So he reported to the unit that Glenn wasn't likely to make it. Stanley survived but couldn't return to duty.

On the fifth day in the hospital while he lay down on his belly, the doctors meticulously picked out the shrapnel out of him and dropped them into a bucket. After several pings, he reached down and picked up a piece of the metal and said, "That looks like an old piece of scrap iron I'd find out on the farm. I'll send that home for a souvenir. My dad wrote back to me and said, 'It looks like an old piece of scrap iron I'd find out here on the farm."

Glenn's urine had tested for an infection, with blood and pus. He was ordered to drink copious amounts of water and take sulpha tablets. The next day he found a generous sample of urine left unattended. So he poured part of it in his cup and marked it with his name. Then he was released, and he returned to his unit. One of his buddies found him a fancy-issued hat that had been lying in a plane, and another gave up his bunk and moved to the chief's quarters. He drew his flight gear, had one of his two-a-day meals, and prepared to make his next flight the day before Christmas. Two out of three days

Glenn flew in whatever plane was available for whatever duty he was called for. Then he volunteered for dive-bombers. Two others chose torpedo planes, and they were killed at the Battle of Midway.

US Naval, National Archives #80
USS Yorktown

"They flew us down to Samoa in B-24s, and then they sent airplanes over from the old *USS Yorktown* just before the Battle of the Coral Sea. It was on the *Yorktown* that I got orders to go up on deck to see the skipper of the ship. Usually, this is not a good thing. I was working in my dungarees with no time to change. Captain Buckmaster was respectful, offered me a chair and a cup of coffee. He recognized me as a survivor of the attack on Pearl Harbor, but he was more interested in what I thought of his son-in-law, Lieutenant Mini. I told him that he seemed to be an all right kind of guy and that we had had no problems. The conversation was brief, but cordial, and then I returned to my duty station. I have to admit the whole conversation was a bit out of the ordinary."

In the spring of 1942, Japan was at the height of its power and control of the Pacific. In the Battle of the Coral Sea, on May 4-8, it was the first time in history that all fighting was done by aircraft carriers. The *USS Lexington* was lost at sea, but they said, "It was amazing not one man was lost during the evacuation of the ship."

The next trial by sea was the Battle of Midway and was the turning point in the war. The Japanese had made the mistake of splitting their massive invasive forces into smaller groups. Glenn was assigned duty aboard the *Yorktown*, but he was airborne when it was hit. The *USS Hornet* and *USS Enterprise* had returned to Pearl Harbor for repairs, supplies, and more seamen and reentered the battles at sea ahead of the *Yorktown*.

Coming out of the Navy yard at Pearl Harbor, the *Yorktown* sailed out to sea after being patched up in seventy-two hours. She actually needed more than six months of repairs. She was "a wild carpenter's dream," but she could handle fighter planes. Glenn volunteered, just like Davy Crockett at the Alamo, "You, you, and you!" One main propeller of the aircraft carrier wouldn't turn, so the ship didn't have her normal speed. She led a separate task group followed by the *USS Astoria* and *USS Portland* and six destroyers back to Midway.

"June 4, at 4:30 a.m. the Japanese reconnaissance planes were sighted by the PBYs, who alerted Army's B-17s. By the time the bombs were released and reached the target, the targets maneuvered out of harm's way. I was ordered aboard number 12 dive-bomber with Ensign Koch (Cook) as pilot.

"We bombed the Japanese aircraft carrier, the *Soryu*, after she had been able to dodge bombs and torpedoes. The *Enterprise* dive-bombers got two Japanese carriers—Akagi and the Kaga. The dive-bombers from the *Enterprise* arrived late after our torpedo planes had been shot down. Our bombers hit the carrier from stem to stern, sinking the ship without time for survivors to come up from below the deck.

"The dive-bombers lucked out and spotted a ship that was following them, and it was moving fast. Again dive-bombers from the *Enterprise* bombed the Soryu from stem to stern. Our planes burned and sunk the *Soryu* when their own bombs and torpedoes exploded. Most of their men were killed because they were down below decks without a chance of getting off before it sunk. While the aircraft from the *Yorktown* were in the air, aircraft from the *Hiryu* hit her, and on June 7, a Japanese submarine sunk the already-wounded aircraft carrier.

"I ended up on Midway Atoll and stayed there for almost a week before returning to Pearl Harbor. There I got survivors' leave, got back to the States, and got married. I was sent back to sea again and served on carriers in dive-bombers until January of 1944. I got orders to come back and go to school for a year. I made chief and got duty on the East Coast, flying off of converted oil tankers. When the war in Europe ended, I got stationed on the beach at a naval air facility in Dahlgren, Virginia.

"Then dispatches came in for all able-bodied, qualified combat airmen to prepare to return to the Pacific. I told my wife to pack up and take our two boys back to her mother's. Then they dropped the two atom bombs. And WWII was over, and I never had to return to the Pacific Theater. I stayed in the Navy until 1969 when I retired as a master chief petty officer. I was in the Korean and Vietnam wars, but I didn't see any combat action.

"After a hiatus of over sixty years, I was awarded the Purple Heart in 2001 by special request. Rep. Rick Larsen assisted in obtaining the long-overdue award. I was awarded the Navy Cross, which is the second highest honor. I was inducted into the Combat Aircrew Man Hall of Fame on October 4, 2002, in Midland, Texas."

At age ninety, Glenn is still active in hunting, fishing, backpacking, a gentleman farmer, cattleman, and is an avid sports fan. On January 26, 2008, Glenn celebrated his ninetieth birthday at the CPO Club. Among those who wished him well were EODMU 11 Commanding Chief Pete Beville, EODMU 11 Commanding Officer Joseph Diguardo, and Lane's daughter Trish Anderson. Mike Gregoire, First Gentleman of Washington State, was present to congratulate Glenn on his birthday. Glenn, you're quite a guy!

Milton Henry Littke

Japanese Prisoner of War

Milton was born January 4, 1920, in Merrill, Wisconsin, to Frank and Emma Littke. His family lived along the Wisconsin River, where his family walked down from their property and fished along the river. Hunting had never been any good, farming didn't bring in enough income, and there were no jobs available. His family had been hit by the Depression. The Littkes came out west to work on a highway bridge near Clatskanie, Oregon. Milton graduated from the Clatskanie High School in 1937. While working in the area, he met his future bride, Mary Ellen. She worked on a farm on Deer Island, which is about thirty-five miles down the Columbia River from Portland, Oregon.

His story had been a repetitious pattern across America during the 1930s. The Depression era preceding WWII had left young men without jobs and opportunities. Many worked in Civilian Conservation Camps wearing old WWI uniforms. Milton, like many others, found work in the Northwest and then enlisted in the military. Milton enlisted in the Navy in Portland, Oregon, on March 12, 1940, and completed his boot camp training in the Naval Training Center (NTC), San Diego, California, and Aircraft Maintenance Mechanic

(AMM) in time to come home for Mary Ellen's high school graduation ceremony. Mary Ellen agreed to wait for his return.

He had been assigned to PAT Wing 10 at Ford Island, Hawaii. It had two squadrons, VP-101 and VP-102. In November of 1940, Milton was deployed for a year to Olongapo in the Philippine Islands. His point of operation was Sangley Point, and Milton was berthed aboard the *USS Langley* (CV-1, later AV-3), the Navy's first aircraft carrier. Guided by Capt. Joseph M. Reeves, he undertook the task of development of carrier operating techniques that were essential to the action in the WWII by supporting seaplane patrols and providing aircraft transportation services.

The Japanese strafed the Philippines on the same date, December 7. December 8, the Marines were under attack on Wake Island in the first hand-to-hand combat battle in WWII. Milton aided in the defense of Cavite and Manila. On December 10, at noon, fifty-four Japanese Betty bombers began virtually destroying the Cavite Naval Yard in the Philippines. In the forty-five minutes that followed, they had delivered a major blow to the defenses of the Philippines.

Approximately twenty-seven thousand or more American civilian prisoners of war (POWs) in World War II would be held by the Japanese during the course of the war. Of the nineteen thousand American civilian internees held in WWII, close to fourteen thousand were captured and interned by Japan. For the United States, the war formally began when Pearl Harbor was attacked.

Milton was one of three mechanics aboard a PBY. On December 14, while on patrol mission, his PBY aircraft crash-landed and was buoyed while another air attack was in progress.

On December 25, Milton left Cavite on a tug that was loaded with every hand it could carry. Passing the eastern tip of Corregidor Island, which guarded the entrance to Manila Bay, they made a run to Mariveles (a small beach port on the southern tip of the Bataan Peninsula and two miles across the channel from Corregidor Island and thirty miles from Cavite). General MacArthur had declared the city of Manila an "open city," which meant it was free of all military personnel and equipment, which left it undefended. At that moment, all military changed into civilian clothes and continued transporting supplies to Corregidor and Bataan.

By December 29, the Japanese stood at the southern gates of the city, unopposed, with orders to destroy everything they could, including all the communication equipment. Others blew up the oil supply depot in Pandacan in the Manila port area. Milton recalls burning all forms of his Navy gear and personal belongings. Among his personal affects to be destroyed were the wedding rings he had purchased for Mary Ellen, his fiancée.

December 31, eight sailors, including Milton, were selected to return to Sangley Point with orders to return with supplies, equipment, and trucks. The following day, the crew departed Sangley and flew over the bridge over the San Fernando River when they met U.S. Army tanks that had been captured and manned by the Japanese. Their aircraft, a PBY, was strafed, and it plunged into the sea. The crew was forced to swim for the beach. The Japanese fighter plane returned to strafe the beach as the crew reached the beach. One of the eight men was killed and another lay dead still until the tanks passed. Milton and five others avoided the bullets that pelted the beach like hail. Then they made their escape into the hills.

"I hid out in caves until about the middle of April with another buddy. We survived with only the clothes on our backs, eating papayas, wild bananas, coconuts, *cahoy* frogs, small fish, and occasionally, rice from the natives. Three Japanese on patrol spotted us fishing and fired shots. I was shot across the lower extremity of my chin. Blood flowed down my face and neck, but they didn't care. I was captured wearing a bloody T-shirt, filthy shorts, long pants, and barefoot, then led back to their jeep. I was suffering from numerous ant and insect bite wounds. I had open ulcers on my arms and legs. The natives had taught us how to treat ourselves for beriberi and variations of trench foot, but I was not without more superficial injuries including the gun shot wound.

"After a long jeep ride to Manila, I was jailed in a hotel without any medical attention. I had to sleep on bare concrete without a blanket. I gave them only my name, rank, and serial number during the four days of interrogation. Then I was sent to a school to learn rudimentary Japanese so that I could follow their commands. I was told to follow their rules, given two blankets and meager food rations that was usually rice.

"I was then interned by the Japanese at Pasay School Prison, Bilibid Prison where I helped with the cooking of a watery soup made from eggplant and *daikons* but mostly water. Sometimes we had some rice for dinner or supper." At Bilibid, there was no sanitation and not enough to eat. The prisoners had to adjust to the overcrowded conditions, camp organization, lack of medical attention, and most significant was the daily agonizing battle to keep the will to stay alive.

"We all felt that our ability to live through the succession of days and nights in this hell came predominately from our being from the smaller communities, farms, ranches, lumber camps, and the Civilian Conservation Camps, rather than the large cities back home. For we had known hunger and bad times, and possessed basic survival skills and with bodies that had already known hard physical labor.

"I worked in the walled city of Manila clearing rubble from the bombings. Then I was assigned duties as a stevedore in the Port of Manila Prison until 1944. Later I was moved to barracks within the pier area with sleeping platforms with thin infested rice mat mattresses. This was luxurious in prison standards: equipped with showers and flush toilets. It was there that I worked with an electrician making tin cups and cookware. We made hot plates from strands of steel cable wrapped around one-fourth-inch wire embedded in clay. The tricky part was getting the desired lengths of wire to produce the desired heat. While imprisoned at Bilibid, I never once received a single letter from home, nor did we get any Red Cross packages. We all felt lost and forgotten as the prison camp began to fill with Allied refugees from battles lost at sea and the islands in the Pacific.

"The benefit of working as a stevedore was the opportunity to occasionally steal a piece of fruit or something else that was edible. That was a risk that some of the POWs were willing to take, but the price of getting caught was a brutal beating, perhaps to death. Many of the infractions seemed minor, such as turning the wrong direction because he didn't understand the Japanese language. The weaker the prisoner, the more severe the beatings were for the infraction of their rules. Inner strength and character was the only difference between death and the will to survive.

"Once a man was hurt, or became sick, the Japanese placed every obstacle in the way of his recovery by withholding the medicines provided by the Red Cross. They weren't issued blankets or fuel to warm the sick quarters, and their rations were reduced. The prisoner usually died as a result. Although the men seldom could expect anything more than a cup of soybean soup and a teacup of steamed rice, the Japanese officials falsified reports, stating that each prisoner received a daily ration of 420 grams of rice, and/or rice and barley, or corn and barley. And that food was plentiful in the Philippines."

On July 17 of 1944, Milton was lined up to be loaded on what was an inter-island freighter before the war. The ship had sailed from Japan to the Philippines, picked up sugar, and returned to Japan. Milton, like thousands of other POWs, was taken by a ferry to the middle of the harbor that was already congested with ships. Milton walked up a gangplank in one of five companies and stayed in his assigned company until the end of the transport. Company 1 sent to the back, then Company 2, and so forth. Those lucky enough to be in the last two companies were a little more fortunate. They saw light from the hatch occasionally. Once the freighter was loaded, the ladder was pulled up, and the hatch shut.

The Japanese sent water down once a day in a big old bucket. Not everyone was fortunate to even get a sip unless a luckier buddy got enough to share. They also sent down a big bucket of food once a day. They designated some American to dole out the soupy rice once a day. As for the latrine, it was an open bucket of human wastes. Unfortunately, when the bucket was hoisted up out of the hatch to be dumped, it usually splashed on the prisoners below. This was entertainment for the Japanese. The prisoners never had a change of clothing. They wore a pair of khaki pants and shirts and one pair of underwear.

"Noto Maru—hell ship—painting"

It was impossible to stretch out and had very little room to sit. The POWs often sat, squatted, or stood back to back for hours in the crowded small ship's hull. Nobody could lie down. There were some that were sick, but there was no medical attention available. And any men who were sick became victims of harassment should the Japanese find out. Tempers would flare once in a while, but that was short-lived. Everyone was litterly in the same dark, unventilated, putrid, stinking boat. Once when they were allowed to mount the ladder up to the deck, the prisoners were sprayed down with ice-cold saltwater from pressure hoses. Then after about ten minutes, they were sent back below into the hold.

"My first order aboard the *Noto Maru* was to throw all my belongings, including my 'new' shoes, into the hold. I hadn't had a pair of shoes until late 1943. Now I had to tie them together and throw them away. With little food or water, we were packed into the stinking hold, which was filthy with coal dust, congealed sugar syrup, even horse manure during a twenty-two-day journey to Moji, Japan."

These hell ships were floating concentration camps on the ocean waves and were not marked as POW transports. Therefore, these ships were often attacked and sunk by the Allied forces by mistake. The cruelty and barbarism was beyond anything that Milton had experienced as a POW. The prisoners were murdered, bayoneted, starved, dehydrated, and suffocated without provocation. Rations dropped into the hold were fought over like ravenous hounds over a rabbit. Those too sick or weak to compete for food steadily grew worse and were victimized by the Japanese guards.

A large number of the hell ships were torpedoed and bombed by Allied aircraft and warships that had no way of telling the freighter was full of prisoners. Most POWs were calm during an Allied attack from above. In fact, many in the hold below were hoping the hell ship would be hit. Once they heard and felt one tremendous explosion and saw a big glare in the sky. That had to have happened when a Japanese tanker was hit. Since they were in the hold, they couldn't see any actual fire. Someone yelled, "Yeah!" The Japanese closed the hatch so the POWs couldn't see anything.

One documented case recorded the Japanese freighter *Arisan Maru* sailed from Manila on October 10, 1944, carrying 1,800 American prisoners, mostly officers. The *USS Snook* sank the freighter *Arisan Maru* on October 14 out in the China Sea. The American submarine had no way of knowing that POWs were aboard. The Japanese destroyers nearby ignored the sinking freighter and those prisoners who were able to escape the sinking hull were murdered by the Japanese crew members. Perhaps ten may have survived. Approximately two hundred names have been registered as Japanese hell ships.

"Our next stop was Taiwan and then to Japan. I completely lost track of time, but I've been told it was August 3 when we arrived in Japan. I remember there was at least one death on this trip to hell. We landed at Moji on Kyushu Island. All the shoes that we had been ordered to tie together were in a huge unmatched pile. Now we were ordered to just find any pair of shoes. Then we were herded aboard a train for Tokyo and trucked into the mountains. Ordered out of the trucks, we had a three-mile hike to Kamioka. I recall vividly that one POW stopped to drink from a ditch. He was hit with the butt end of a rifle and told to get back in line. No other POW dared to come to the aid of another. Any act of charity usually resulted in decapitation or bayoneting of the Good Samaritan.

"The camp was not sanitary. The camp was already overcrowded with other American, British, Dutch, and native Javanese prisoners as slaves for the Mitsui Mining Company until September 4, 1945. We slept on straw mats without necessary blankets. The only source of heat was a small wooden box containing a meager amount of charcoal. Most of the POWs had dengue, beriberi, and dysentery. The guards made it as miserable as possible for those who were sick, in hopes of reducing the prison population. I remember having one bath during the entire time I was in this camp, which was at least a year. We had to dig our own latrines and remove the snow from the roof of our barracks.

"I worked in the lead mines for nine hours each day. At times I worked the conveyor buckets. Any ill or injured prisoner was forced to finish his shift or risk being beaten to death. Our work was inspected every day, and reports were sent to the mining company. On the way to work, I would pick vegetation and eat it or boil it later to make a tea. This is where my initial experiences of living in caves with the help of the natives for three months before my capture paid off.

"We were allowed ten cigarettes per week if you were healthy, which I once traded two for the shinbone of a horse. I boiled it repeatedly and drank the broth. Then I roasted it in a fire to gnaw on until that sixteen-inch bone was down to four inches. Only then it was discarded. We ate nothing but cooked rice and maize. About once a month, we were given a small source of protein (fish, soybeans, or meat) as a reward. But we never received any mail or Red Cross packages until the war was over.

"On August 15, 1945, we didn't get called to work. This wasn't the usual one of the occasional Sundays that we got off. It was two days later that we were told that the war was over. We celebrated by pooling our meager savings and bought a horse to eat. It wasn't until September 4 that a plane flew overhead and dropped Red Cross packages, but we never saw any U.S. troops.

"It was the Japanese that took us to Tokyo on flatcars and turned us over to the Americans. It took a few days to load about 1,600 ex-prisoners aboard the *USS Ozark* and we headed for the Guam Fleet Hospital.

"On September 12, I weighed in at the hospital at 136 pounds. I was then transported on October 2 to United States Naval Hospital in Oakland, California. Then I was transported to the Naval Hospital in Astoria, Oregon, arriving on the seventh. I took leave from there, without knowing that my family was not notified by the military until the previous day that I was even alive after five long years. Although I had sent a cablegram through the Red Cross prior to leaving Tokyo, I was home before the cablegram arrived, and no one was home to greet me. Not a single grateful American stopped or smiled to greet me during my homecoming.

"I was almost back to my normal weight in the hospital when I started walking toward home. Apparently, the day before, my

parents had gone to pick up my sweetheart, Mary Ellen. She had waited those five long years for me, not even knowing whether I was still alive or not.

"At least my family was thrilled by my return from hell. We were married on October 21. I had replaced the wedding bands and engagement ring that I had been forced to throw into the sea with my other personal belongings.

"Within a month, my life had changed so much on the surface. But we knew nothing of post-traumatic syndrome back then. I wasn't able to deal with all the horrific memories. My family had no way of understanding what hellish mental souvenirs were buried in my soul. No one wanted to talk about it, and neither did I. There are too many horrific mental pictures that still haunt me. Sometimes I found a little peace out in the woods near our house. Other times I just felt like the tears would not stop. However, I stayed in the Navy until my retirement on March 8, 1960, after twenty years of service to my country. I retired from active duty as a Navy Chief at Whidbey."

Milton and Mary Ellen still resent the fact that more than twenty-seven thousand POWs were held by Japanese and those who suffered and survived every conceivable violation of the standards for the humane treatment of POWs established at the Geneva Conference. That it took sixty years to be awarded his Purple Heart. Where were the ticker tape parades, brass bands, magazine photographers, or flags waving to greet the weary and wounded home on the west coast?

Furthermore, in the Pacific Theater, the death rate was 37 percent, and among the POWs captured in Philippines, the rate was 40 percent. While less than 6 percent of our veterans remain living, the debate still rages over suing the Japanese corporations and the government of Japan for wages for slave labor during the five years of WWII and compensation for the citing of violations of both The Hague and Geneva Conventions.

He currently resides in Oak Harbor with his wife, Mary Ellen. The Littkes feel that "our own government and the Veterans Administration have been grievously incompetent and unappreciative of the abuse our surviving soldiers and sailors suffered at the hands of the Japanese. They failed to fight for the compensation due us for the enslavement and cruelty forced upon those Allied POWs held by the Japanese. The Japanese violated every code of decency established by the Geneva Conference without consequence. Will our government, like the Japanese, just wait for us to die and be eternally silenced? So it is only by sharing a chapter of my story that future generations know what has been left out of American history textbooks."

Let's hope that WWII historians and our government archivists wake up and listen to your plea so that Americans may honor WWII Japanese POWs veterans.

God Bless you, Milton.

Harry Hackett Ferrier

WWII and Mutual Assured Destruction

Harry Hackett Ferrier was born in Springfield, Massachusetts, January 23, 1925. At the age of sixteen, he enlisted in the U.S. Navy on January 28, 1941. The Ferrier family had been having more than their share of life's trials during the Depression era. His mother had remarried after the death of his father when he was thirteen. Now living with an alcoholic stepfather, times were challenging for his sisters, Jacqueline and Virginia, his brother, Robert, and half brother, Richard. The next three years were difficult, yet he persevered through these hard times. Harry thought seriously about joining the Navy as soon as possible and the prospect of flying as a Navy crewman generated excitement and motivation for him.

Harry states, "After recruit training at Newport, Rhode Island, I was assigned to Aviation Radio School at Jacksonville, Florida. In early September, I had been assigned further training in Torpedo Squadron 8 (VT-8) in Norfolk, Virginia. This air group would be assigned to the brand-new aircraft carrier *USS Hornet* (CV-8). My first experience as a crew member was in the Douglas TBD-1 Devastator; that was the Navy's first all-metal monoplane shipboard aircraft.

"I knew we were preparing for the possibility of war. The British couldn't have been less prepared. It wasn't unusual for the British war machine to resort to using old biplanes and WWI destroyers. These were desperate times for the British, and Canada seemed to be their only ally. President Roosevelt and Congress were still calculating whether our country would voluntarily get involved in the war in

Europe. I was more interested in how my part in all this talk of war would play out for me.

"In spite of all the training, Harry and the other young recruits would not be prepared for the consequences of President Roosevelt's radio announcement on December 7, 1941. Our country was not prepared any more than Western Europe for a second world war. I had been going home on leave from Virginia to Springfield, Massachusetts, by train. My mother met me at the door when I arrived home for my leave. President Roosevelt's declaration of war meant I must leave immediately for Virginia. Furthermore, my brief encounter gave me just enough time to tell my mother and family good-bye. We all knew that I might not ever see them again.

"The *USS Hornet* made her first shakedown cruise before proceeding to the Pacific. I was to continue my personal and intensive military preparation for war at NAS Norfolk, Virginia. In March of '42, I actually visited the Grumman factory to learn as much as possible about the new Avenger from the people who designed and built the airplane. The new Grumman TBF-1 Avenger torpedo planes proved to be extremely stable, rugged, and roomy. A torpedo plane flew as low as one hundred feet off of the water at the designated target. The plane was to get within a thousand feet of the enemy vessel and release the torpedo, which was self-propelled with its own built-in engine. The pilot had to determine where the course of the torpedo and the enemy ship would eventually intersect. Once released, the torpedo sank approximately fifteen feet under the surface of the water and would run its course toward the enemy target. Success was a direct hit.

"Then the pilot and I went to Rhode Island in mid-May to practice dropping torpedoes out over Narragansett Bay. We wanted to evaluate the plane's performance during and after dropping the torpedoes. Our pilots found the Avenger simple to master despite its dangerous mission of boring in on enemy ships at water level while under anti-aircraft fire. The Avenger carried three crewmen: the pilot, the radio operator/gunner, and a turret gunner (or sometimes a bombardier). Our group at the receiving detail was ordered to fly the new planes to California. Then we were loaded onto a transport headed for Hawaii.

"The *USS Hornet* had already left the port a day prior to our arrival for an unidentified destination. Then the six Avenger planes took flight to aid in the defense of the Midway Atoll. The seven-and-one-half-hour flight covered 1,100 miles of the Pacific Ocean. This was the premier maiden voyage for our pilot, Ensign Albert 'Bert' Earnest, USNR, who had never flown out of sight of land before this day. Jay Manning was our turret gunner. We reached the Midway Atoll on June 1, 1942, where the long-range fuel tank was exchanged for a two thousand-pound torpedo.

"The Navy had been able to break the Japanese's code and knew the intentions of the enemy. At the Midway Atoll, we had three carriers, and the Japanese had four. On June 4, our Avengers took off from the Midway Atoll ready to rumble against the Japanese carrier force. In retrospect, we were confident, but very naive, thinking that our new airplanes were quite superior to the enemy's aircraft. We were assigned a job, and I didn't think in terms of what facing combat conditions would be like."

Within three days, Harry would be facing mortal combat and all the typical human anxieties that thousands of others had before their first combat experience. At 0600, on June 4, six TBFs were launched from the Midway Atoll. The attack was scheduled for 0700. The enemy carriers had been located by patrol aircraft (PBY Catalinas) on a bearing of 320 degrees, 150 miles from the Midway Atoll. Torpedo Squadron 8 was divided into two groups with fifteen Douglas TBD-1 Devastators on the *Hornet*.

The six brand-new Grumman Avengers launched from the Midway Atoll were all intercepted by a large group of Japanese Zero fighters as they approached their designated target, the Japanese carriers. This was Harry's first experience of aerial combat, and the pending results would become a naval disaster for the innovative Avenger torpedo planes. The pilot had used the intercom to report that he could see the Japanese fleet on the horizon. The tail turret gunner reported that they were under fire. It was impossible for Harry to defend the aircraft with a .30-caliber machine gun from below the tail; because of a hydraulic failure, the tail wheel dropped down. The gun was useless when he tried to shoot down the attacking Zero. Over his shoulder, Harry saw that their turret gunner, Jay Manning, had been killed when the attack began. Harry was left with the responsibility of defending the aircraft.

Ignoring hot liquid on his wrist, Harry was down on his knees manning his gun and too busy to give it his attention. He remembers coming to; the scalp wound sustained from machine gun fire continued to bleed onto his face and eyes. Harry had no concept how much time had passed. During this furious combat with the Zeros, their aircraft sustained sixty-four machine gun and nine cannon shell hits. Harry had the good sense to notify his pilot that he was still alive and request permission to crawl up the seat nearer the pilot.

"I had total confidence in the pilot. I couldn't see, so I must have been responding by instinct."

Both pilot Ensign Ernest and Radioman Ferrier had been wounded in battle. Earnest managed to regain control of the plane after being under attack by two Japanese fighter pilots. He had lost control of the plane because his elevator control had been severed, and the airplane was trimmed nose down. Then the pilot opened his bomb doors manually to release the torpedo and prepared for a water landing. Instinctively, he reached down, rolled the trim tab, and that brought the nose up so he could get the airplane flying on course again. He had lost his compass, but he had flown west to engage the enemy; therefore, he flew south initially to get away from the Japanese. Then he used the sun as his compass until he saw smoke on the horizon. Then they knew that it was Kurri Island, and the Midway Atoll was about fifty miles away.

"If they had expected cheers and a warm welcome, any emotions of relief dissipated quickly. On the Midway Atoll, the deck crew waved him off when he approached the landing strip and then again on his second approach. They could see that the landing gear wasn't correct, and they tried to radio the pilot to bail out. The pilot couldn't hear anything on the radio. He could feel the runway and brought her down roughly third time at a reduced airspeed anyway. The starboard wing dropped down on the landing strip, and the plane spun around. The impact was of no real concern until the plane grounded to a halt and looped off the runway.

"I raised the canopy and climbed out on the wing after the landing. Any landing you can walk away from is a good landing. This had been a good landing. But we certainly had a more realistic revelation of the horrors of combat."

Meanwhile, the main body of the VT-8 had launched from the *USS Hornet* and commenced their attack at 1000. All fifteen of their TBD-1s were shot down during the attack; only Ensign George Gay survived and was rescued from the Pacific waters the next day. Altogether, VT-8 lost forty-five of the forty-eight pilots and crew members in the battle. There were only three who survived. *Harry was the only crewman and he survived a shot to the head.* That may have been a blessing as the Zero fighter planes may have assumed he was already dead, as did his pilot. But not Harry; he lived to see more combat. Harry's baseball cap had been returned to him the next day, but he never wore it again. As tragic as these death tolls were, it was the turning point in the Pacific War. The Japanese Navy's plans to include occupation of the Midway Atoll failed. Yamamoto had split his massive invasion force into small groups, and it would be his undoing. From now on, the U.S. Navy would dominate the Pacific once the new U.S. carriers arrived.

Following the Battle of Midway, Harry went back to Hawaii aboard a marine airplane and received retraining before he was reassigned to the Torpedo Squadron 3, VT-3. Except for two former enlisted pilots, the squadron was decimated at the Battle of Midway. Like Harry's squadron, of the twenty-one planes, only two pilots and one radio operator returned. Only three survivors out of forty-two crew members who flew into combat that morning to face the Japanese Naval fleet returned.

After July 15, 1942, Harry would be flying with Ensign Fred Mears from the *Enterprise* for a series of battles beginning on August 7 during the invasion of Guadalcanal. Later, the Japanese attacked three combined American task forces under the command of Vice Admiral Frank J. Fletcher, aircraft carriers: *USS Saratoga, USS Enterprise,* and *USS Wasp,* equipped with a total of 254 aircraft.

On August 24, the American Marines prepared a limited offensive to eliminate the Japanese pressure on the western flank of their beachhead. The Avengers were sent out to protect the Marines landing on Guadalcanal. They were trying to keep the Zeros away from the Marines. Unfortunately, Japanese dive-bombers attacked and damaged the *Enterprise;* three bomb hits had disabled the aft elevator and destroyed the starboard aft five-inch gun battery. Altogether, eighty-six men were killed and later buried at sea. The Avengers had been away from the ship when it was attacked and were lucky enough to be able to return aboard the *Enterprise.* Those aircraft still in the air were given orders to stay away while the force was under fire. Their .30-caliber guns in the nose of their planes were useless in this kind of antiaircraft combat.

Five VT-3 Avengers had been detached from the *Enterprise* to operate from the Henderson Airfield on Guadalcanal. The *Enterprise* returned to Hawaii for repairs. Torpedo Squadron-8 was reunited with the pilots and crews of the VT-3 Avengers a few days later. The VT-8's ship, the *Saratoga*, had been torpedoed and put out of action and headed toward Hawaii for repairs.

"I was reunited with Ensign Ernest, and we continued to fly numerous daily missions in support of the U.S. Marines on a daily basis. On a rotating basis, we were to target and bomb Japanese transport carriers and lure the Zeros away from the U.S. Naval and Marine forces for three weeks."

While the war in Coral Sea continued, the combined squadrons returned to the states and were decommissioned in December 1942. Harry was granted a thirty-day combat leave that gave him an opportunity to travel home to Springfield, Massachusetts, by train. Then in January of 1943, Harry was newly assigned to the Bombing Squadron 5 (VB-5) aboard the new carrier *USS Yorktown* (CV-10) under the command of Jockco Clark. During the shakedown cruise of the *Yorktown*, the first SB2C-2 Hellcat aircraft built by Curtiss-Wright proved to be inadequate for combat. So deficient were these aircraft Commanding Officer Jockco Clark had the planes immediately removed from the *Yorktown*. Harry reported to El Centro, California, for training on the Douglas SBD Dauntless. The *Yorktown* had passed through the Panama Canal, and Harry was back aboard and headed for more combat in the Pacific Theater.

Photo # NH 95571 VB-5 SBDs aboard USS Yorktown, April 1942

Photo # 80-G-17061   USS Yorktown being abandoned, 4 June 1942

While his squadron was assigned to the *Yorktown* in August of 1943, Harry flew numerous combat missions aboard the Douglas SBD Dauntless airplanes. The squadron received a total of ten battle stars for their actions in the Pacific Theater during 1943-1944. From Harry's perspective, none of the twelve combat situations since his first in the Battle of the Midway had been as horrific as the first.

"I volunteered for the new bomb squadron. I felt more comfortable aboard a dive-bomber than the Avenger torpedo plane. I was now the radioman/gunner for senior pilots with more combat experience. On April 1, 1944, I was appointed chief petty officer at age nineteen, which was crazy. Then I received a commission as an ensign when I reenlisted in January of 1945 while assigned to VC-33. As an ensign, I was known as a 'mustang' because I had crossed the line between enlisted and commissioned officer. Now I was in a training command, teaching the Navy's coding system for reporting enemy sightings until August 14, 1945, when Japan surrendered, and the war was over.

"June of 1946, I chose to revert back to chief petty officer so that I could continue to fly. I felt more at home while flying again. Then I was transferred to the training command as a communication instructor for ten-man aircrew flying the PB4Y-2 Consolidated Privateer Aircraft in Opalocka near Miami, Florida."

Addendum

Harry became a hurricane hunter for four hurricane seasons (long before satellite meteorology technology advancements) in the Atlantic, the Caribbean, and the Gulf of Mexico. Now flying in a modified PB4Y-2 that had a dome in which the aerographer could make his observations, he recalls one particular hurricane reconnaissance flight off the East Coast. Because of the extended size of the storm, they had flown too far east. After jettisoning all their loose gear and two empty bomb bay fuel cells, they landed at a Coast Guard air station with only ninety gallons of fuel remaining in the tanks.

Harry's naval career resumed when he was in Maryland and given his commission back when the Korean War erupted. While others served our country in the Korean War in Korea, Harry was assigned duties in the Nuclear Weapons Program. He was trained as an aviation electronics officer in Memphis, Tennessee.

"In September of 1952, I taught young soldiers, sailors, and airmen in Albuquerque, New Mexico, how the trigger mechanism was going to work for exploding an atomic bomb assignment, I was sent to Nevada twice to observe the atmospheric nuclear weapons tests. I became an instructor and an escort for VIPs who came to survey the potential destruction of atmospheric nuclear weapons. This was all part of the military buildup during cold war between the U.S. and the Soviet Union or the MAD Program (Mutual Assured Destruction)."

WWII, nuclear testing in Nevada, and Vietnam—of the three, Harry has been most emotionally affected by his role in Vietnam. At age seventeen, he was naive about combat and bravely followed the orders given to him by his superior officers and did his job. Twenty years later, he made *three combat cruises* providing support for the amphibious assaults by the U.S. Marines on the shores of Vietnam. In September 1964, Harry stood aboard the *USS Princeton*, LPH-5, helicopter carrier, for two years as an officer watching a new generation of confident and naive youngsters hit the beaches only to return in body bags. Supplies were transported by helicopters and returned with wounded and the casualties of war. According to Harry, watching from the deck was the hardest assignment he ever had to complete during his career in the U.S. Navy. Ironically, this was the first combat duty in which Comdr. Harry Hackett Ferrier felt the mixture of self-confidence and distress of being a "real U.S. naval officer" pulsating in his veins while on the command deck of the *Princeton*. He had completed his jobs admirably and retired in September of 1970 with the rank of naval commander and went into public service.

His military decorations include the Distinguished Flying Cross, Purple Heart, the Air Medal, four Presidential Unit Citations, and several Theater of Operation medals and awards. Commander Ferrier was honored in 1997 by being inducted in the Combat Aircrew Roll of Honor at the *USS Yorktown* Aircraft Carrier Museum. The flight crew from the Battle of Midway was honored in 1998 by being inducted into the Confederate Air Force's American Combat Airman Hall of Fame in Midland, Texas. The World War II Veterans Committee awarded him the Chester Nimitz Award for Distinguished Service in the U.S. Navy during World War II at its 2003 conference.

"In the spring of 1998, I accompanied Dr. Robert Ballard in the search for the *Yorktown*, CV-5, that was sunk at the Battle of Midway. I appeared in two television movies. First, on the Discovery Channel in a movie titled *Midway* that aired in 1999. The National Geographic Society was one of the sponsors of the trip and commissioned the explorer movie *The Battle for Midway* that was also released in 1999."

December 2007, at a reunion in Fredericksburg, Texas, the National Museum of the Pacific War, "Turning Points—Midway and Guadalcanal" featured leading historians who discussed the pivotal points in the U.S. victories in the Pacific. Harry met a Japanese Zero pilot, Kaname Harada, who shot down two TBFs from the Torpedo Squadron-8 detachment based on Midway Atoll. According to these historians, it is in all likelihood that it was Harada who had wounded Harry in the heat of the Battle of Midway. Harry still has the sixty-five-year-old baseball cap, with the bullet hole, as a souvenir of his first combat mission in the Pacific Theater. Who would have thought such miracles happen—two "youngsters" who were mortal enemies in 1942 would stand together, arm in arm, in 2007.

Harold Johnson

The Seaman with a First-Class Angel

Harold Johnson was on born on Puget Sound Island, twenty-five miles west of Longview, Washington, and the widest part of the Columbia River. His father was Olaf K. Johnson, and mother was Anna M. Nelson Johnson. He attended first grade in Puget Island, then went to school in Oak Harbor for two years. Then they moved to Bellingham, quit school, and joined the Navy at age seventeen.

"I joined the Navy, on April 1, 1941, because ships always used to come in to the harbor there, and as kids, we used to go down and get free rides on the boats. Then we went to Gedunks for ice cream cones or candy bars. My dad had lost the family farm, so he became a commercial fisherman. There were times when he had to live with our grandparents on Whidbey Island. My older brother was fishing while the rest of us kids stayed in Whidbey Island. It seemed like my father and mother were always looking for work during the Depression years.

"Two things really stick in my mind about boot camp. One is we used to have 'watches.' Of course, the only thing we had to watch was the clothesline. We called it 'clothesline watch.' I had the midwatch with a rifle, leggings, belt, bayonet, etc. We had to march back and forth in front of the clothesline. It was about midnight, and no one was around, so I started whistling.

"Suddenly, there was a tap on my shoulder, and a Chief was standing there.

He turned me around and said, 'What are you doing, sailor?'

"I was standing watch, sir!'

"What are you doing besides that?"

"I'm whistling."

"There are only two people in the Navy who whistle: one is the bos'n's mate, and the other is a damn fool. And you're not a bos'n's mate."

"So he put me up against mast-like pole where the clothesline came down from the peak of it.

"I want you to stand here and whistle the rest of your watch."

"He came around and checked on me to make sure that I was whistling. Pretty soon nothing would come out. My cheeks were sore from trying to whistle.

"The next time someone else had done something wrong, the whole company suffered. At midnight, they gathered all of us together, and we had to get our sea bags, roll up our hammock, and put it around our sea bag, put them both on our shoulders. Then we went out for a run around the grinder four to five times with 135 pounds of equipment on our backs.

"After boot camp, I requested a battleship, and I was assigned to the *USS Oklahoma*. I reported in at San Francisco Bay. Boy that was a big ship. It looked to me like a pretty ship sitting out there in the bay. They could launch planes right off it where it was anchored. And that was my first experience: I saw a plane being launched and taking off. It was so impressive.

"I was assigned to the Fourth Division, number 4 turret handling room, which was the powder room, to send power to the main guns up on the elevator. My quarters were on the port aft side. We had fold-up bunks, four bunks to a tier and other bunks on the other side. We took meals right in our quarters with fold-down mess tables and fold-down legs hanging from the overhead. Otherwise, it was pretty comfortable. Reveille was about 0600, and the mess cook brought coffee around to everybody. Then we would go up on the main deck and scrub it down with holy-stones.

"Our part of the deck was the starboard side, and the Fifth Division had the port side. A sailor would wash down the deck and get it all wet. Then a bos'n's mate would sprinkle sand and lye on the deck. We had a brick or stone with a hole in it, and we'd put a stick in the hole and rub sand and lye up and down the deck. A guy with a big hose washed it down behind us. It was bleached out by the lye and so clean that we could have eaten right off the deck. Our other duties were to paint and polish brass the ship's 'bright work.'

"When I went aboard, the ship was in San Francisco Bay for shaft repairs. So I was there for about two weeks waiting to go into Hunter's Point to get a new shaft. While the ship was in to dry dock, we scraped the bottom and painted the bottom and sides before heading out to sea for Pearl Harbor.

"At Pearl Harbor we went on maneuvers four times. One time we rammed the *USS Arizona*. I'm not sure whose fault it was, but one of the ships made a wrong turn during blackout maneuvers at night. We rammed the *Arizona* into something else and put a hole in her side and buggered up our bow, so we were in dry dock for another two weeks. On another time we were on maneuvers, we were almost rammed by the carrier *USS Enterprise*. I was on watch on the mainmast, and I could see the *Enterprise,* and it looked like it was going to ram us amidships. I was looking right straight down on the flight deck. As it just made a turn and we turned, it clipped our stern flagpole off. I don't know if that was the last mistake we made during maneuvers or not. I do know that the Japanese subs were spying on our maneuvers through their periscopes.

"We had just come back from a week of these maneuvers the first week of December. I went on liberty every chance I got. In fact, I had a date scheduled for the December 7 with a pretty little Hawaiian girl. I spent some time at my favorite little restaurant, The Black Cat, a tavern with the best food in town. Of course, I was too young to drink, but did anyhow."

Harold Johnson, a seaman second class at age seventeen, cleaned up and got ready for the Sunday or holiday routine in Pearl Harbor. The uniform of the day was tropical shorts and a T-shirt. He had spent most of the week working in the mess hall or "holy-stoning the wood decks" of the *Oklahoma*.

"This was to be liberty day, and I was getting ready to meet my date on the beach until the alarm rang out to 'man your battle stations!' At first, the alarm was interpreted as an unwelcome drill. Everybody started squawking about having a drill on a liberty day. Suddenly, death and destruction ripped through the skies, sinking or damaging 18 warships, destroying 180 aircraft, and killing at least 2,400 Americans. 'It was no bull, but the real thing!'

"It felt like the whole ship jumped out of the water when the first torpedo hit. The Marines were below us and came running up through their hatch, and everyone ran to their battle stations. There was a hatch right where I was running down the passageway to number 4 turret. Water was coming down from the first torpedo, got on my arm. I thought it was mustard gas and rubbed it. The pain only got worse. When I got to the handling room, my arm burned like fury.

"I was part of the magazine crew at battle station, had been the number 4 turret gun. They had been heaving powder bags that were elevated up the shaft behind the projectile. The barrels of these guns were fourteen inches in diameter and would have been effective if the *Oklahoma* had stabilized. But the power failed as she slipped into a forty-five-degree angle and continued to slowly roll over.

"Four other torpedoes had hit their target, and the emergency lights dimmed, and she started going over pretty fast. Oil had been spilled on the steel deck by someone, and a lot of the guys couldn't make it. The lights came back on momentarily. I was given a helping hand up the ladder by the bos'n's mate standing there. Only one guy made it up the ladder in front of me when the lights went out and stayed out! Somewhere going up the ladders, I got ahead of him. The ship continued to roll over as crewmen tried to jump over each other. Others clung to air while rolling with the ship. My division officer, Lieutenant Junior Grade Spitler, was already on the deck hanging on to the hatch as the *Oklahoma* rolled over. I jumped on top of him, grabbed him around his waist. Another guy jumped on top of me. Then it was getting to the point where I couldn't go up the deck, the ship had rolled over too far. I decided to swim for it.

"Those overboard were trying to swim through six-to seven-inch layer of oil that was now leaking from the *USS West Virginia*. The flames from the bow would soon set the whole area ablaze. I spotted a seaplane from the deck of the *Oklahoma* turn over in the water. I grabbed a hold of the pontoon and hung on. Oil was on the water six to seven inches thick and caught fire. Others were holding on to the keel of a motor launch that had turned over. Japanese planes were strafing them, peeling wood off the motor launch. It was a long time before boats from the submarine base came over to pick us up. I didn't recognize anyone because they were all covered with oil. Once they were washed down with aviation gas at the base and washed again, only then were they allowed to shower, and then issued clothes and shoes. Every time somebody saw a plane or heard an unfamiliar antigun fire, they thought the Japanese were landing on the beach.

"I think it is fair to say that we couldn't believe what was happening. We were all in shock. That evening, we mustered to see who was who. During the night, the guys heard noises, saw airplanes that weren't there, antiaircraft guns took off after shadows. I didn't sleep at all that night. I was always thinking that the Japanese were landing on the beach.

"Most of the turret crew topside got out, about ten from the turret, five of us got out of the magazine and about twenty more from the handling room. The rest were trapped down there. Some of the guys were forced to go back down by an officer and/or petty officer who told them to go back down. I was lucky I got up the hatch and ladder because the water was almost ready to come through the overhead hatch."

Only 300 of the crew of 1,300 on the flagship *Arizona* survived the blinding flash from the bomb dropped directly down her funnel. The only battleship, the *USS Nevada*, in 'Battleship Row,' was intentionally beached to avoid blocking the channel. The *West Virginia* took most of the beating, protecting the *USS Tennessee*. The *Oklahoma* took most of the nine torpedo hits protecting the *USS Maryland*. Then slowly capsized and flipped over. The *USS California* was scuttled and later raised, repaired, and returned to active duty."

His first-class angel showed him the light from the hatch cover on the upper deck, and he managed to climb the inclining ladder. Hal saw his division officer, Lieutenant Junior Grade Spitler, hanging on the other side of the hatch cover. With a crew of 1,200, 32 were cut out of the hold of ship the following day, and 429 went down with the ship. The *Oklahoma* remained capsized for the next three years. The *Tennessee* and the *Maryland* were later towed to Bremerton, Washington.

"The next afternoon our division officer, Herb Rommel, got us all together out there with the muster list. Later he called us out again, and we were already assigned to other ships. I went to the *USS Worden*, destroyer 352. I was assigned to the radio shack to start with.

"The *Worden*'s first engagement was the Battle of the Coral Sea. In early 1942, the *Worden* accompanied the *USS Lexington* and the task force. Unfortunately, the *Lexington* succumbed to massive internal explosions and fires started during the battle. About one-half of the crew was lost before they abandoned the carrier. We picked up the tanker *Tippecanoe*, a real old WWI tanker, which had just gotten done fueling all the ships in the fleet. We escorted it and a cruiser that went along with us that picked up most of the survivors back to New Hebrides, taking another four days.

"After returning to Hawaii for supplies and repairs, the *Worden* screening the *Enterprise*, we headed for the Midway. We saw the *USS Yorktown* headed for the American Islands of Midway. They had broken the Japanese code. This would be the turning point in the war for the U.S. Navy. But the cost was high. The *Yorktown* was hit. The flames and smoke buried the ship at sea. The *Enterprise* carrier, in spite of the glaring floodlights like a Christmas tree on the deck all night, tried to get all the Navy torpedo or fighter planes back in case they were lost. But none came back. The fighting had been done in the air, and the U.S. Navy had prevailed.

"After Midway, we went back to Pearl Harbor. We got overnight liberty, and about five of us missed the ship. In order to get overnight liberty, we had to know someone on the beach who was married to vouch for us. We really planned to stay at the YMCA, but waiting for us was a message about our ship preparing to leave. So we called our friend who had vouched for us, but he had already gone back to the ship. It was blackout, so no jitney or taxi would take us out. When we got there, the ship was going out the bay. Then we went aboard the *Whitney*, a destroyer tender.

"Then in a couple days, we got assigned to a marine transport that was going to Guadalcanal. I sailed on that and worked in the officer's mess cooking. I had good meals for the first time in a long time. When we got to Guadalcanal, the invasion was just underway. We loaded Marines in boats and sent them over on the beach. Then brought back the wounded and dead, and we had some burials at sea for the Marines. I had watch on a 20 mm gun that night when the big battleship, the *Nagata*, engaged in the big sea battle with its task force. We lost three cruisers and the Australian cruiser *Canberra*, the cruisers *Astoria*, *Vincennes*, and *Quincy*. I had a front-row seat to the battle. I could tell who was firing. When the Japanese battleship was firing, the whole silhouette lit up, and I could tell what it was. I could tell when the cruisers fired back. The silhouettes were right there.

"One reason we lost ships was because it was a battleship, *Nagata* with sixteen-inch guns, was fighting cruisers with eight-inch guns—a big difference. The task force could have come in there and sunk the whole works—about one hundred ships in the harbor—but they turned around and left us. I remember during the battle, the day before, we had all these tanks, jeeps, trucks loaded on booms and ready to go in the water with LSMs and landing craft. And that night, they cut everything loose so we could get underway if we had to. Brand-new jeeps, trucks, and everything went into the drink.

"The day after the battle, one of the cruisers, either the *USS San Diego* or *USS Oakland*, took the five of us aboard and out to our task force. The old *USS Saratoga* was being refueled from a tanker, and the *Saratoga* was refueling the *Worden*. We were transferred back to the *Worden*, whose crew had been starving and had run out of fresh stores. They had been eating rotting stores for about two weeks. Many of the personnel were skinny, malnourished, and ill. I was court-martialed and busted back to the deck force."

Following the victories at Coral Sea and Midway, the Marines launched their first attack in late 1942 on Guadalcanal, in the Solomon

Islands. The *Worden* screened the *Saratoga* as the carrier launched air strikes. Their efforts, together with those of the cruisers and destroyers, provided the coordinated shore bombardment, which covered twenty thousand Marines. Her orders were to screen the supply and communication lines leading to Guadalcanal. The invasion of Guadalcanal was costly; the fighting that followed this invasion was some of the bloodiest in the war. The *Worden* was war weary, and so was her crew. But Harold's first-class angel stuck by him through all those daily air raids.

Once again, the *Worden* headed for Mare Island, California, for a major overhaul. Harold got a thirty-day leave, which he spent with his parents in Bellingham, Washington, and his grandparents Mr. and Mrs. John Bell on Whidbey Island. Too soon he was back in San Francisco, on the destroyer, in the Pacific, and heading north to Alaska.

USS *Worden*: Destroyer

The Japanese had turned their attention on Alaska. Dutch Harbor had been bombed, and the Japanese now occupied two of the Aleutian Islands. The *Worden* arrived in Dutch Harbor by New Year's Day with additional troops and supplies amid atrocious weather conditions. She had escorted the *USS Arthur Middleton* to guard the Coast Guard troop transporter on her maiden voyage from San Francisco to the Gulf of Alaska in weather so stormy that heavy waves washed over her stern. That night a williwaw came up.

The *Worden* screened farther out into the Constantine Harbor and was dashed onto the rocks. On January 12, a sudden strong current dashed the *Worden* onto a pinnacle that ripped her hull beneath the engine room. Without power, or safety cables, enraged waves smashed her against the stony shoreline. She beached and broke up in the stormy surf. "Abandon ship," bellowed Comdr. W.M. Pogue before he was swept overboard and knocked unconscious. The destroyer rolled on her side on the rocks with mammoth waves breaking over her. She had broken in two, with sailors and officers alike were holding on to the stern section.

USS *Arthur Middleton*: Coast Guard Troop Transport

Landing boats from the *Middleton* and *Worden*'s sister ship, the *USS Dewey*, were filled to the gills with her crewmen aboard. It only took ten to fifteen seconds in the freezing water before they died from hypothermia. It was extremely difficult to pull a man out of the water. Fingers tore into freezing flesh. Once aboard, their frozen clothes were quickly removed with a sharp knife while they were propped up against the wall, then wrapped in warm towels and sent to the infirmary.

"Like Commander Pogue, I had survived another disaster at sea. The destroyer sunk in the freezing waters of the strait. Twenty seamen were lost at sea due to hypothermia and injuries. I felt like I had won the lottery! Three weeks' survivors' leave, a free trip to the Caribbean and Florida, and behind door number 3 was submarine-chasing school. You can't chase submarines without a boat. The grand prize was the sweetest little ship I had ever been on, a 150-foot U.S. PC-462.

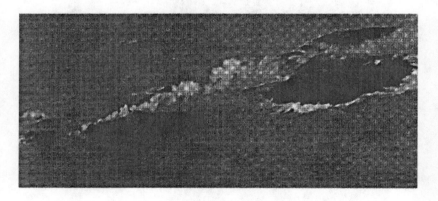

"I spent a year on this sleek craft escorting convoys, rescuing ships that had been torpedoed in the Caribbean waters between Cuba and the Panama Canal. We dropped mines on enemy submarines and guarded the U.S. merchant ships bringing aircraft parts from the west coast to the factories on the east coast. In 1943, newer ships were being sent into the Pacific and the older ships were being sent to the Atlantic Ocean through the Panama Canal.

"In the Pacific Theater, the ground troops were taking a beating. More soldiers, pilots, planes, and landing ship tanks (LST) were needed there. I would be on board the LST 668 in 1944. I saw combat for the next six months on the seas between New Guinea in Southeast

Asia and the Philippines and then on to Okinawa. I remember how intense the fighting on the island was. The U.S. Navy and the Army Air Corps shot so many rounds of bullets in the air at Japanese bombers that their own ammo fell back down on them like rain on the ocean waves. It was during this time three thousand kamikaze planes bombed and sank thirty-six Allied forces' ships. The war was not over!"

His first-class angel had seen Harold through more than any man's share of combat. So she arranged for Harold, now a Bos'n's mate, first class, to see home again in July 1945 after two eventful years of overseas duty.

He lived as a civilian until 1950 when Harold was called back to active duty during the Korean War.

"They shipped us over there, and a bunch of ships were lend-leased to Russia, and they gave them back to us and left them in a mess in Yokosuka, Japan. We put them back in commission. They were patrol frigates with three-inch guns. They were such a mess that it took a long time to make them seaworthy again. Most of our duties were patrolling the Korean Coast (*USS Hoquiam*—PF5) up the rivers and shooting mines and such. Then we'd fire at the beach with our three-inch guns.

"That was war far different than WWII because we were only allotted two rounds from each gun every two hours to the beach. We were up this river, and they knew when we were going to fire, so they'd hide and wait. When we were done, they'd come out doing their thing and fire small firearms at us. They couldn't reach us. We'd shoot mines that they would float down the river. We'd stand watch and shoot them as they came by. That was one of our patrol duties.

"Our home port was Yokosuka. We'd go back and clean up. Images of WWII came back for me when I recognized the guy running the yard crew was one Japanese ex-admiral, whose flag was on the battleship *Nagato* that came into Guadalcanal and sunk our cruisers. I think his name was Vice Admiral Gunichi Mikawa, too hard for us to pronounce, so we call him Admiral Sam. Three of us got to know him pretty well. We would go over to his place. His house was very traditional. We sat at a low table on cushions with our feet underneath being kept warm by a heater. After serving us our meal, his wife would leave us to talk about the war. When he was an admiral, he was a chubby little guy with medals all over his chest, and when he was at the shipyard, he was a skinny little old guy.

"Every time that our ship came in, he was right there. He kind of adopted us. Admiral Sam hadn't gone through the war trials, most likely because he had picked up U.S. Navy survivors from the Battle of Guadalcanal and saved their lives."

Admiral Sam's work crew in Yokosuka

"If you're going to join the Navy, you'd better be a good swimmer!" Good advice from a brave seaman who swam through hell so that he could come home to heaven—Whidbey Island.

Robert "Bob" S. Biddle

Athlete, Warrior, Hawkeye

There's an obvious pattern of Bob Biddle having demonstrated the keen eye and a steady hand of both an athlete and a warrior. The display of tributes to Bob praises him for his innate athletic ability to excel as a fast softball pitcher, for being an exceptional bowler, a hole-in-one golfer, a competitive volleyball player, and a commercial pilot.

On further inspection also displayed are tributes to the warrior side of Bob's nature: three Distinguished Flying Cross citations, seven Air Medals, two Navy Unit Commendations, four Good Conduct Medals, Korean Theater Medal, Asiatic-Pacific Campaign Medal, plus two battle stars, Combat Air Crew Wings this is correct with three battle stars—which represent on land, sea and, air—and American Theater Victory Medal. To his family and friends, he's recognized fondly as Bombardier Bob because he was inducted into the Enlisted Combat Aircrew Roll of Honor aboard the *USS Yorktown* in 1999.

Bob was a student at Phoenix Union, the only high school in Phoenix. He entered the ROTC program as a private. By the end of his sophomore year, he was a captain. Then he joined the Arizona National Guard Medical Detachment with an all-Native American unit out of the Indian school in Phoenix, Arizona. While in this unit, Bob served as the company medic. The Indians were all noncoms and tribal chieftains. The officers were all white, but the only way to get anything done was to go to the tribal chiefs who were privates. In 1940, Bob and the unit, known as the Arizona Bushmasters (an aggressive venomous snake found in Panama), went on maneuvers in Louisiana. They had a reputation as being the toughest-fighting combat team that General MacArthur had ever seen and chose the Arizona Bushmasters to lead his return to the Philippines.

"Ironically, I was 'kicked out' before the regiment was nationalized and went regular Army. I was only sixteen years of age and two years too young to be enlisted in the Army. However, I received an 'Honorable Discharge for Fraudulent Enlistment' with a character reference as 'excellent.' At the legal age of seventeen, I reenlisted in the Navy on 4 September 1941.

"After I finished recruit training in San Diego, I arrived in Seattle, Washington, on the USS *Saratoga* (CV3), sleeping in a hammock instead of a bunk. When the Japanese struck Pearl Harbor, the *Saratoga* was in the Bremerton shipyards. I had joined a Navy squadron that flew PBY5s until the PBY5A (*A* for *amphibian*) arrived. After the war broke out, the squadron was sent to Tongue Point, Oregon, for sub patrol on the peninsula west of Portland. My commanding officer, LCDR James Russell (later to become Admiral Russell), predicted the Japanese would strike along the Aleutian chain within ten days. The squadron headed for Kodiak without me.

"Pearl Harbor and Dutch Harbor were the only U.S. coastal defenses on the Pacific Rim. Both the U.S. and Russia considered the Aleutians mere stepping stones to coastlines of the other. After finishing torpedo school, I arrived aboard on old seaplane tender (AVP12) in the Aleutians the midnight just before the Japanese bombed Dutch Harbor on Unalaska Island on June 3-4, 1942. The fifteen Japanese dive-bombers damaged an American ship, hit several petrol tanks, and killed forty-three servicemen. The two-day battle over Dutch Harbor threatened the Naval Operating Base, which included the air station, submarine base, ship repair facility, and facilities for provisioning the fleet.

"After the 'all clear' signal, I had intentions of running down to see if my PBY-5As survived when I ran across three young men in a machine gun emplacement who had been strafed and killed. This was my first exposure with death. I confiscated a rifle and a bandolier of ammunition. I emptied the rounds of ammo on the Japanese at Dutch Harbor. Months later, my crew and I moved to Cold Bay and lived in tents and Quonset huts. Fort Randall boasted that it had become the strategic air base having the longest runway. Twenty thousand personnel supported that base, but I had enough of Cold Bay, Adak, and Uminak. I left my fresh salmon slow cooked around a campfire. I was assigned to Air Bomber School in San Diego. As a bombardier instructor in NAS San Diego, California, I had a lot of fun flying in a Slow Navy Bomber (SNB) bomb trainer for half the day. The other half I was instructing trainees to use the Norden bombsites

Then, I joined the Patrol Bombing Squadron, VPB 121, and assigned to Air Crew One (Commander Pflum, skipper). The PB4Y-2 Privateer was a four-engine bomber. There were twelve planes in the squadron.

Usually, only one to three flew a mission. In February of 1945, we flew missions between Hawaii and Midway on a anti-submarine chase, then on to Eniwetok in the Marshall Islands.

"From Eniwetok, we bombed Wake Island. Known as the Alamo of the Pacific, it was well armed, and their mission was to keep the runways torn up so the Japanese couldn't refuel or repair planes used to attack the Marianas. VPB 121, flying the PB4Y-2 Privateer, dropped a record number of bombs on Wake Island.

"On our first mission, we had lost a wing-man. His plane blew up. I had trained most of the squadron's bombardiers, and I recognized this as a loss due to a technical error. The pilot took their plane to a 16,000 altitude, then immediately dropped back down at 200 mph to 14,000 feet or diving to the deck. This maneuver was called the 'glide bomb.' The bombardiers used the Norden bombsites to drop their payload on target. While the Japanese had guns aimed at the highest altitude, the squadron was already at a lower altitude and dropping bombs before the Japanese knew what hit them. The pilots would 'jink left or right' to get away from the flak. Once the captain of the squadron approved this maneuver, the missions were far more successful. I may have preferred to fly with another pilot, but the captain wouldn't have it any other way. I was his bombardier.

"Keep the enemy runway on Wake Island torn up!" That was the routine every other day. Every other night, the Japanese would fill the previous craters. So 'the beat went on' until I talked with the ordinance officer on Eniwetok about delayed fuses. Together we determined it was

possible to drop a bomb with a delayed fuse that would detonate six, twelve, or twenty-four hours later. Should anyone, friend or foe, jam the fuse or try to disengage the arming mechanism of the bomb, it would immediately explode. I shared my strategy with the captain, and he agreed. Only I was to set these delayed arming mechanisms. Our new strategy ended the runway game of 'bomb and fill.' The Japanese didn't want to play anymore."

His squadron moved to the island of Tinian in the Marianas until it was secured. The squadron advanced until they were now flying out of Iwo Jima at low altitudes to Japan. Cruising at a low altitude of 1,500 feet made the crew more vulnerable and tense. Bob had a new nickname: Hawkeye. As the name implies, Bob could see an object or a target a mere 50 feet above or on the water. He had binoculars, and a glass bonsai was his window of opportunity. Bob had clear vision ahead and on either side of the plane. When he spotted a target, he let the captain know, and the plane would zip up to a 300 feet, then increase speed to 200 mph and glide to 100 feet so that the top turret gunner above and nose turret had visual contact. Should they miss, Bob had visual contact for backup. Using this technique, Bob sank sixteen Japanese ships, one bomb per ship for which he was put into the Ordinance Hall of Fame and his captain received the Navy Cross.

"Once we were able to save the pilot of a P-51 afloat in the South Coast of Honshu. We called for a rescue submarine. Meanwhile a nine-hundred-ton Japanese ship was headed for the floating pilot. I dropped two five-hundred-pound bombs, one at each end. I blew it out of the water. The Japanese had tried to sink the rescue submarine as it crashed-dived but managed to miss it. Japanese Zeroes and P-51s fighter planes were 'dog fighting' overhead. One of the P-51s went down in flames, the other three P-51s, running low on fuel, left for the base on Iwo Jima. The remaining enemy was flying between two of the PB4Y-2s so they couldn't hit him. Our plane overtook the floatplane and shot it down. The engine exploded like a loaded cigar, the pilot stood up, the plane plummeted, and he bailed by flipping over backwards off the tail of the Zero without a parachute in sight."

Addendum

Post-WWII, Bob remained in the Navy and served in Korea. Somewhere in his naval career, Bombardier Bob developed a wicked fast ninety-mile-per-hour underhanded softball pitch. Bob pitched for three years with a record of seventy-two wins and only three defeats at Ream Field in San Diego.

The Navy composite team of all-stars defeated the East Coast All-Stars two out of three games. The NAS Memphis, Tennessee, team played numerous "barnstorming" tournaments from Arkansas to Florida during the year he was stationed in Tennessee as a bombing instructor. Bob polished off his twenty-year naval career at NAS Whidbey. He served his community as an Oak Harbor policeman, Island Co. deputy sheriff, worked for the Oak Harbor School District, worked at a dude ranch in Southern Arizona. Bob is a charter member of the PBY Memorial Foundation and board member. Someday Bob will consider retirement.

It would be a generous gesture of gratitude to every veteran who fought in the Pacific Theater if each and every one who reads this article and remembers their favorite veteran will send a $10 donation to the PBY Memorial Fund, PO Box 941, Oak Harbor, WA 98277.

Lawrence "Doc" Dykers

"No War Was Ever Fought That the Infantry Didn't Have to Clean It Up"

Lawrence "Doc" Dykers was a modest WWII veteran who left his construction job, friends, and family here in Oak Harbor, Washington, at age twenty-five as a draftee in the U.S. Army before the Japanese bombed Pearl Harbor. Doc's brothers Obert and Chapin stayed home to run the family farm; his sister Barbara Dykers would become a Navy nurse seeing action in the Pacific, Iceland, and England as Lieutenant Commander Dykers, retired from her career in the Navy as a commander. Sisters Martha and Gertrude and his mother sent supportive letters and the latest Whidbey Island gossip to Doc and Barbara regularly.

Lawrence Dykers was born December 19, 1916, and graduated from Oak Harbor's high school. He attended college in Pullman, Washington, for two years. There he earned the nickname Doc, which has stuck to him better than any of the Band-Aids he always carried around in his pockets. Because he had been required to become a fully trained member of the WSU ROTC program, Uncle Sam tapped Doc on the shoulder and said, "We want you!"

"I entered the Army infantry at Fort Lewis, Washington. I stayed only six months in the Eightieth Army Infantry Division at Fort Patrick Henry, Virginia, before being issued 'taped stripes' on my uniform. I was sent to Officer Candidate School at Fort Benning, Georgia. On July 15, 1942, Maj. Gen. John E. Sloan, commander of the U.S. Fifth Army, reactivated the Eighty-eighth Infantry with a promise to WWI veterans to get the job done. Most of the recruits were young, green, and didn't begin their formal training until August 3, 1942. Major General Clark was a strict disciplinarian and a stickler for minute details, but he got the results he desired. I too was young and naive.

"Now a second lieutenant, I met up with my old friend Jim Ronhaar, an Army engineer from Oak Harbor, at another intersection of our lives. At Fort Sam Houston, Texas, I also crossed paths with Brig. Gen. Paul Kendall. Brigadier General Kendall severely reprimanded me for 'helping' a young recruit from Kentucky try and improve his scores for marksmanship. Brigadier General Kendall gave me an earful that I never have forgotten. We would meet again.

"Under the command of Lt. Gen. Mark W. Clark, the 88th Division of the 350th Infantry left Fort Sam Houston for the Strait of Gibraltar and on to Casablanca, French Morocco, on December 15, 1943. Then our division was moved to Magenta, Algeria, after Christmas for intensive training. I found myself in the first division of draftees to be sent overseas.

"The Eighty-eighth Division arrived overseas with about fourteen thousand men. Brigadier General Kendall was the first member of the Eighty-eighth Division to set foot on Italian soil. Lieutenant General Clark dispensed orders for me to set up the camp, deal with the Italians, question prisoners of war, and establish a protocol for sending the captured POWs to the rear and then to the POW camps in the U.S. It was not unusual for voluntary surrender by the POWs for want of food.

"Maj. Gen. John E. Sloan ordered strategic training in the Atlas Mountains. The training paid off, not only was the Eighty-eighth in top physical condition, they were prepared for the wintry terrain that lay along the 'boot' of Italy. The Fifth Army was trying to get to Cassino and gain control of the central highway to Rome. It arrived at Naples, Italy, February 6, 1944, and concentrated in the Piedmontd'Alife area for combat training. An advanced unit went into the line before Cassino, on February 27, and the entire unit relieved the British unit.

"The Eighty-eighth Division also had orders to 'move on up the boot,' get supplies, food, and fuel to the troops at the front line. My unit was one of only two that ran strictly on mule power. Very few of the soldiers in my unit had any experience with mules. Orders were orders, and forty-five to sixty mules had to be tethered together with heavy packs that hauled ammunition, K rations, supplies, and mail to our troops. These mules were vulnerable to the Italians who wanted them for farm stock, and the Germans wanted the supplies and food. Both were the U.S. mules' worst enemy.

"The men in the Eighty-eighth Division at the front line were weary, exhausted, and not used to the higher altitude. For any chance of survival, we kept twenty-four-hour-a-day vigils for snipers and smaller groups of Germans that were well hidden in the rough ridges. It was while I was on one of these treks that I was shot in the right hand and was hospitalized in Livorno. This was the first of two gunshot wounds I would get in Italy. A platoon leader in my regiment, Charley Lynch, made several visits to the hospital to check on my recovery. Charley's father was Col. Peter Lynch, but Charley and I called him Colonel Pete. Of the three hundred thousand in the Eighty-eighth, these two buddies would survive.

"When the U.S. Army occupied Corsica, Livorno (Leghorn), and the Port of Naples—areas recently controlled by the German forces—they fled for higher ground. On May 11, the Eighty-eighth drove north to take Signo, Mt. Civita, Itri, Fondi, and Roccagorga, and reached Anzio. When more U.S. troops arrived at the invasion of Anzio, the two fronts linked up. On June 4, after a stiff engagement on the perimeter of the city, they advanced into Rome.

"Charley Rich, a devoted Catholic, had been able to slip into Rome undercover. He invited me to go with him to see the pope. We met Pope Pius XII. I was a Protestant. It didn't seem to matter to him. I still received metal medallion and a blessing for a quick recovery of my wounds to my right hand. I would need that blessing in the coming months of combat.

"The Germans held a tenacious grip on the mountain passes after retreating north of the Arno River. They set up defenses north of Rome along the backbone of the northern Apennine Mountains and resisted further advancement bitterly. Unknowingly, at least two Whidbey Islanders from Oak Harbor were in Rome on June 4.

Unfortunately, both the Fifth and the Eighth armies were depleted and exhausted when other units were pulled out for the invasion of Normandy and Southern France. One member of those units pulled out of Italy when the Allied forces took Rome was Wes Zylstra, from Oak Harbor. Wes was now in the newly formed Seventh Army Infantry under the command of General Patch and on his way to the invasion of southwestern France.

"Brigadier General Kendall's arrival made everyone nervous, including me. When I heard that Brigadier General Kendall planned to accompany me on one of those dangerous treks to deliver the supplies, I had hoped that Brigadier General Kendall had forgotten our first encounter at Fort Sam Houston, Texas. No such luck, Brigadier General Kendall had a knack for remembering faces and details. After returning from our trip, I was surprised to find out from Brigadier General Kendall, he was there to inform me that I was now First Lieutenant Dykers. I remember these events with some fondness, and I take pride in having served my country.

"After a period of rest and training, the division, under the command of Capt. Robert Roeder, opened its assault on the Gothic Line on September 21, taking Mt. Battaglia on the twenty-eighth. We fought the 'Green Devils' of the German First Parachute Division. Capt. Robert Roeder had commanded our company in defense of Mt. Battaglia. The 350th arrived slightly ahead of Eighty-eight Division, and we were readily introduced to some intense and desperate hand-to-hand combat with the Germans. The enemy fought just as savagely, and the fighting would continue on into the Po Valley. Shortly after taking occupation of a strategic position, Capt. Roeder continually circulated amongst the troops to encourage them.

The peak of Monte Battaglia after the stand by Company G.
American dead still lies in the foreground.

"We had grown up with similar family values. As a commanding officer, Capt. Roeder was a pretty fair guy. The whole company had a sense of solidarity with one another. I remember that he wrote many letters back home to his girl in Pennsylvania. I was the company finance officer, so when the men in our company sent money, I sent it home for them.

"The men of Company G rallied to drive the enemy off the summit and back down the slopes of Mt. Battaglia. At night Capt. Roeder checked his men in their foxholes, but at some point, he had been wounded by the enemy during his rounds. I will always wish that I had tagged along that night to cover his back.

"In the morning, he was found and immediately carried to the command post. Knowing that he was dying, Capt. Roeder gave me orders to brace him up in the doorway. He began shooting his weapon and shouting words of encouragement to his unit up until the moment he died. I was one of those who carried his body to the medics, but it was too late. I had lost my best friend. Without a moment to grieve the devastating loss of my best buddy, I became the unit's only surviving commanding officer. Within the next seven days, all the other officers of Company G would be killed or wounded, and the unit would be reduced to fifty men.

"I quote from the authorized Citation by the War Department, General Order 10, 1945, 'In the face of incessant and violent counterattacks by powerful enemy forces. Artillery and mortar barrages preceded each attack; then each was climaxed by bitter firefights, bayonet charges and grenade duels. The gallant officers and men of this battalion repulsed each attack with a marked display of fighting ability and teamwork.'

"I tried to encourage the weary warriors to remember Capt. Roeder and force back the enemy. Teams of litter bearers courageously transported the wounded long distances through artillery barrages. When our unit was out of ammunition and grenades, they threw rocks at the enemy or resorted to hand-to-hand combat. As the remainder of our unit waited for further orders and the kitchen outfit to arrive, a couple soldiers and I left the front line to search for fresh ammunition. The Italians had been too afraid to bring it the rest of the way up the mountain, had abandoned the supply mules during the battle. We found several mules still with supplies and ammunition in their packs. Fortunately, I had taken with me a boy from Kentucky who also knew how to handle mules, and we were able to round up most of mules and take them back up the mountain.

"We had new orders to fall back from the front line and let fresh replacements continue pushing the retreating Germans on the front line toward Po Valley. What was left of our 350th fell back for a much-needed rest and medical attention. After this fierce mountain action, the regiment was nicknamed the Battle Mountain Regiment. But it was Axis Sally during her broadcasts in Berlin who gave our 88th Infantry Division the nickname Blue Devils. Between September 26, 1944, and October 5, 1944, the 88th Division's three regiments sustained 2,105 casualties, 1,420 of them in the 350th Infantry alone.

"Each night we had to be wary of snipers and armed. Yet hungry Germans implored us that they would surrender for food. During one night in particular, I had dug my own foxhole without the aid of my Italian boy who routinely dug foxholes for the Americans. When German fighter plane suddenly strafed the camp, I took shrapnel in my lower back. Although I was ambulatory, I spent ninety days in the huge ward of other wounded in a hospital in Rome.

"Because of my wounds, I had to be reassigned when I went before the Higher Rank Officers Board, through which all orders were dispensed. I was assigned to the fire department of the Fifteenth Army Air Corps. I had orders to take ten trucks and forty men and move the fire department on Corsica inland. We were to protect the four-inch pipeline that carried the precious aircraft fuel. I may not have been out on the front lines again, but our unit was constantly kept busy putting out fires started by Italians who were trying to steal the fuel. Both our unit and the Italians were under attack from German snipers. Most of the fires were caused by careless and cigarette-smoking Italians. Our orders were to get that aircraft fuel to the Army Air Corps of B-17 and B-24 bomber squads in such bases as Manduria, Foggia, and Bari. No excuses!"

The men and mules of the Eighty-eighth Division had successfully taken Italy from the Germans step-by-step over rugged terrain that made machines, tanks, and jeeps useless. By May 2, 1945, when the war in Europe ended, Doc had earned the Silver Star for Courage under Fire, the Bronze Star for Bravery, a Purple Heart, and a gold cluster for the second significant wound. Numerous ribbons for marksmanship, good conduct accompany the Unit Citation for Gallantry, Valor, and Bravery.

Doc shares this thought, "Any good infantryman should always dig his foxhole deep enough to cover his assets." He still carries pieces of the shrapnel in his lower back, and to this day, he sets off the bells and whistles if he tries to go through airport security. After the war ended, he exchanged letters with other buddies in upstate New York, South Dakota, and Pennsylvania until their deaths.

Doc returned home to Whidbey Island and a better way of living outside of foxholes. He took a job as a mail carrier and met the love of his life on a blind date introduction. Dick Tullis had slyly introduced Doc to Doris, and they were married in 1947, celebrating their sixtieth wedding anniversary last year.

If Doc looks familiar to you, he may have been your mailman early in his postwar career; until becoming the Oak Harbor postmaster before his retirement to his favorite rocking chair. Doc served his country and community well. Doc passed away April 29, 2009.

Virginia Madeline Wells

Red Cross Volunteer

Virginia Madeline Wells was a product of the Depression era, but the circumstances in which she was raised were exceptional. The younger sister of her brother Erwin "Scotty" Wells by two years, she was born in Brawley, California, in 1922. Her father, a dentist, had a clientele that provided a substantial family income. Virginia remembers that there were always laborers around her house to wait on the family. Her father absolutely adored her mother. They often entertained in a grand fashion while most of America's population was looking for a meal.

Virginia remembers having maids, cooks, and elegant dinners for elaborately clad guests. She recalls that her family never seemed to lack for anything. She was not aware of the plight of other families. Her father's income had been provided by patients who usually paid with fresh farm produce. Therefore, the family always had food on the table. Her father had set aside enough of his income to send both Erwin and Virginia to college. Things suddenly changed for the Wells family without warning.

On May 19, 1940, an earthquake hit Imperial Valley, California, with a magnitude of 7.1, killing nine people in the area. Literally, their elegant home was shaken from its foundation by the quake. Her father's dentistry office required all of the family's savings to rebuild his dental office. The family's lifestyle changed significantly. Virginia had been a student at San Diego State Teachers' College and found it necessary to use her experiences as a former student of dance to teach dance to others. She finished a four-year program in three and one-half years and became a student resident advisor at the college for Mrs. Southworth. This fortunate twist of fate gave her several opportunities to make a difference in others' lives.

"Mrs. Southworth may have been our housemother, but it was my dorm window that often rattled with the tapping of pebbles late at night or early morning. My own roommate, Mary Beth Cook, often dated my brother, Erwin Scotty. She arrived back at the dorm late on a regular basis. I had been dating a friend of Scotty's, Erwin. It seemed ironic that the boys had the same first name. Scotty and Erwin were both students at a merchant marine academy. Scotty often brought Erwin Horn home. We all always enjoyed chatting about religion and world politics in our family. When Erwin was sent out on his ship for a short workup, Virginia's feelings changed things for both of them.

"I found I truly missed Erwin's company, and the void in me sparked our courtship. He and I spent many hours chaperoned while we cuddled up together on the porch swing. Upon his return, our conversations on the porch became more serious. Erwin Horn's father, a Lutheran minister, helped us plan our wedding in his sister's home before he was due to leave for the Atlantic. We shared a ten-day honeymoon before he packed his things for the last time, and Erwin kissed me good-bye. Technically, Scott and Erwin never graduated from the academy before they were certificated and called to duty. Each of them was assigned to separate merchant ships in the Pacific Theater.

"In the meantime, I signed up as a Red Cross volunteer. The new Mrs. Mary Beth Cook Wells and Mrs. Virginia Madeline Wells Horn had little knowledge where their husbands were or whether they were at great risk. Letters were censored and/or never arrived intact. Being a positive person, I always believed that he would come home. I received one letter from my husband that was nearly two years old. Then my landlord delivered a telegram from the War Department that shook my world. 'We regret to inform you that your husband, Erwin Horn, was killed during a Japanese kamikaze attack.' I returned to my home in Oakland, California, but I had little time to mourn my young lost husband. I was spending too much time feeling sorry for myself. I had to get back to the job I chose to do for my country."

The petite redhead, dressed in her official Red Cross volunteer uniform, admits that she was too foolhardy to be afraid. Virginia may have been naive, but she was good at her job as an ambulance driver.

"Because there were no men available, that is anyone who drove and had a driver's license," explained Virginia.

"I remember one time in San Francisco I had to drive a huge big van full of band instruments from camp to camp. It was necessary for me to parallel-park on one of the hills. The sergeant that accompanied me on these excursions was a 'very large' man who couldn't help laughing uproariously over my predicament.

"I drove up and over the curb onto the sidewalk and couldn't park the Red Cross ambulance. His laughing at me didn't lessen my embarrassment. When I found the humor in my situation, I started laughing as well. Then we couldn't get the van running again. We finally parked it on the sidewalk. Someone put some blocks behind the tires so it wouldn't move.

"The producer decided that I had worked hard enough at this, so they invited me to see the show from the prestigious 'Angel Box' in the second balcony where the bigwigs came and looked over the edge to see everything. It was one of the most memorable times I experienced.

"One of the VIPs seated near me asked me to explain to them what was going on. They weren't interested in the program, they wanted information and answers to their questions about the war. Most of the questions had to do with what I was doing or how I got my job.

"Then someone from beneath the balcony heard me talking and yelled out, 'Louder!' During the intermission, several of the people in the audience were curious to see a Red Cross volunteer. Perhaps they were even more inquisitive as to what I knew about who was where and what was happening. In a short time, I had gathered an audience waiting to ask questions. If they asked me a direct question regarding pertinent information that I felt I could disclose, I answered them. If I didn't feel that I had anything I could tell them, I said so. Soon when they figured out I didn't either know much or wasn't talking. They drifted off in another direction.'Loose lips sink ships.'That was the code for everyone. Anyone who didn't abide by those conditions was subject to suspension as a Red Cross volunteer.

"The job required that drivers had to be able to keep their mouths shut. There were two main categories of passengers. Many of them were military VIPs with titles being transported between San Francisco and San Diego, and then to be transported to or from the Pacific Theater. I don't recall anyone in particular, but many of them sported a lot of brass on their uniforms. Some were probably calling the shots and were headed to the Pacific to follow or give orders as planned. I never knew, nor was I curious. I just concentrated on doing my job correctly.

"On one occasion, I had an ambulance full of high-ranking military personnel when I found out that I had driven to the wrong part of town. There were areas in both San Diego and San Francisco which had suddenly become populated with enemy sympathizers. If they had known whom I had aboard my Red Cross ambulance, it would have been a national travesty, had we been stopped or captured by enemy sympathizers.

"Other passengers were often patients who had medical appointments. Many of them were burdened with mental and psychological wounds, which they were not shy about sharing. Many of them told me stories of what they had been doing, what they had seen, and where they were going. They often asked me what I thought and what I had to say. I had to reply, 'I am not permitted to comment. I am under restrictions to talk about anything about the war.' I was never sure about their stability or if they might just take out a weapon and use it. Some of them were being committed or moved to another hospital for various treatments.

"I don't think I was ever afraid when I was told to do something. I just did as I was told. I'm sure I was not different from the young men who were called to duty. They probably did as they were told. I drove some days in San Diego and others in San Francisco. I was quite busy because the commanding officers could trust me to deliver someone or something according to their orders. It wasn't always safe to drive in areas that had been deemed safe before. I sometimes had to change the route to avoid confronting some gangs-held neighborhoods.

"Many conflicts emerged over women. Servicemen complained that all young men should be in the service. (In fact, many were too young.) But deep down inside, the issue was ethnicity. Servicemen tended to view Mexican Americans as 'foreigners.' By the summer of 1943, soldiers and sailors would cruise into Mexican neighborhoods with baseball bats and broken bottles and beat up Hispanics. Local law enforcement generally looked the other way, and many Anglo-Americans—Angelenos—cheered on the servicemen. The military declared Los Angeles 'off-limits' to military personnel, and the riots calmed down.

"I looked forward to each day. I tried to practice common sense and measure the gut feelings of my passengers as well. Usually the directions were given to me by a single voice. But when they sensed a dangerous situation, they too were aware of the wrong turn. The sergeant beside me and the servicemen in the backseat pointed, communicated with nudges, and held their breaths. Until we were out of the ticklish situation, I tried not to dwell on the danger or the silent conversation going on in the rear of the van. I had made a commitment as a young widow to serve my country in a capacity that was important and a real challenge.

"On one particular assignment, I picked up a group of naval officers at the bus station and delivered them to their quarters. I received calls from the officers to be driven to the USO clubs all the time. A couple of the officers seemed to enjoy the sights of San Francisco and often specifically requested my Red Cross ambulance services. Both of the officers developed an enjoyment for flirting with me, and it wasn't long before I was inviting them both home for dinner. My father always enjoyed cooking a huge barbecue for young people on the back porch. It wasn't long before Al Miller and his buddy Daniel were regulars at my dad's parties. My parents took a liking to Daniel, but Al was much more persistent.

"The war had ended in the European Theater, and Japan was being hammered by our bombers. Tokyo had been a U.S. military target since March and had already been devastated. Throughout the summer of 1945, the Japanese forces held on at the cost of numerous lives on both sides. They continued to resist or surrender while the Manhattan Project continued to develop the bombs equivalent to twenty thousand tons of TNT. While the Japanese were losing the war, back home in California, Al was winning his battle. Al and I were soon sitting on the porch swing, making plans for a wedding.

"After the war, Al was stationed in Japan. I volunteered again. I taught conversational English to Japanese male-dominated classes for approximately four years. There were very few women in any of my classes. Most of my students were businessmen. They weren't interested in educating their women. Al was stationed on the base, but we actually lived in base housing built for the officers and their families.

"I felt our marriage was a nice and warm relationship, and I am grateful for the children we had together: a daughter, Francis 'Lynn,' and a son, Daniel Alan. Besides my love for my children, I continued to work at sharing my passion for teaching. I was active in the Whidbey Playhouse when Al was previously stationed at NAS Whidbey Island. My daughter, Lynn, and I have enjoyed traveling to numerous countries before and after my retirement from teaching in the Oak Harbor School District."

Her memories as a Red Cross volunteer are a treasure for those of who continue to appreciate the devotion millions of Americans had for our country during WWII.

Dorothy "Dot" Virginia Sheehan and Kenneth Carl "Casey" Baier

Tough, Gifted, and Independent

Born November 23, 1921, Dorothy "Dot" Virginia Sheehan's family lived in Dallas, Oregon, when her dad left his two-month-old daughter, older sister by two years, Patricia. Their mother had to take her two babies and move back home to her parents in Omaha, Nebraska.

"At the age of eight, I found a violin for $8 in the Sears catalog. I learned to play my first instrument. My mother remarried to a farmer after her divorce. When she remarried, the family increased with two younger brothers before the Sanford family decided to move to Meridian, Idaho, when I was in the second grade. Mr. Sanford was a farmer at heart and wanted to go back to working with the earth. Many of the farms in Nebraska became a part of the dust bowl during the Depression. I remember some good times when I had my violin, my dolls, all of whom I named Rosalie, and my only Christmas gift was a box of dominoes.

"I graduated from Boise High School before attending college where I excelled in music. I continued my violin studies and played in high school, college symphony, and the orchestra. After two years of college, I taught in a little country school. Then I went back to college for another year to finish and get a degree in music. I played the violin in the Boise College String Symphony and the String Quartet.

"I also won the Southern Idaho Table Tennis Championship. My mother hadn't approved of the competition and wouldn't let me take the family car (which I had started driving since the age of twelve). During my freshman year and determined to compete, I got up early on the day of the competition and rode my bike thirty miles, rested briefly, won the championship, and rode home sound asleep in the back of a pickup that night.

"I have to say my youth had made me tough and an independent thinker. I had decided to take my stepfather's name."

Dorothy "Dot" Sheehan-Stanford does not fit into the typical women's lib image. In her youth, she stepped into a man's world in WWII like many of the women in America.

"When so many men had been serving in the military, ironically it gave women like me new career opportunities. I chose to leave my teacher job, which ultimately led me to being the first woman to drop a bomb from an airplane, using the then top secret Norden bombsite. They weren't sure that women could learn to do it, you see," she replied with a smile.

"At the age of twenty-two, I joined the WAVES (Women Accepted for Volunteer Service) in 1943. That was just a year after they were established in July 1942. I had graduated from Boise Junior College, taught Music and PD, one year in Fairfield, Idaho, before I decided to do my part for the war effort. I guess I helped prove to the powers that be that yes, women could learn to do it. I

did well on my aptitude tests. I had to choose between meteorology school, which I really wanted, and aerial gunnery. Gunnery won out. I graduated at the top of my class Three other women who were also former teachers were next invited to participate in an experiment to see if we women were capable of learning to use the Norden bombsite, then the most sophisticated, top secret bomb-dropping device. Since women did not go into combat then, the object was to train the men who actually flew the planes in the war zone and drop a bomb from an airplane, making me the Navy's first female bombardier.

"I thought the WAVES uniform was nice looking and then convinced me that I should join. The WAVES wore white blouses and Navy pants, and I wanted to do something in bombardiering."

During the war, women, like Dot, took on the challenge of doing jobs that neither men nor women had ever thought possible. When so many men had been away serving in the military, ironically Dot and other women took on the new opportunities.

Dot was one of forty women sent to boot camp at Hunter in New York, New York, for six weeks. Always musically talented, she joined the "Singing Platoon" and participated in a program that was led by the famous director Leopold Stokowski. Music has always a big part of her life, and she is an accomplished violin and viola musician.

"I was sent to the Aerial Gunnery School in Pensacola, Florida, where I learned to shoot and dismantle .30- and .50-caliber machine guns. I was also taught how to use a movie projector which would assist in teaching bombardier students to shoot at moving targets. I was one of four women chosen to be sent to Banana River Naval Air Station, near Coco, Florida, to become part of an experimental group called Air Bombers Training Unit. There we were taught the use of the Norden bombsite, which was so secret, that an armed guard walked with another man carrying it, and it was kept in a vault.

"It was very interesting, challenging because it was a lot more complicated than you would think. It involved working out a mathematical problem with wind speed, altitude, and setting it in the bombsite. Then, with the plane on automatic pilot, the bombardier would use both hands to control the direction of the plane and release bombs over the target. Hard as it is now to use the latest version of the bombsites by Norden, there were no computers at all during WWII.

"The training unit flew in an SBN Beechcraft designed with a Plexiglas nose. The first time up, with the parachute strapped in place, the pilot tossed a coin, and I won the toss. I really got excited then, knowing that I would be the first woman to take on this responsibility! The bombardier sat in the nose where the bombsite was located. I made my way to it, clipped the parachute on, and went to work. I knew that the target was painted on the sand at Cape Canaveral.

"The only thing around it then was an old lighthouse, so the target was easy to see. The plane flew eight thousand-to ten thousand-feet altitude, and I completed my job. Then I dropped the bomb. I had already caged the gyroscope so that the pilot could then take evasive action as if it were a real bomb run.

"Most of my Navy student bombardiers would be assigned to a naval squad in the Pacific Theater. The program was discontinued in early 1945 when the Norden bombsite was phased out in favor of the dropping bombs from higher flying planes."

Dorothy was transferred back to the Aerial Gunnery School, and she would eventually meet Kenneth Carl "Casey" Baier, a first-class aviation electrician.

* * *

Casey had been sent to boot camp in San Diego, California, before being sent for training in Pennsylvania before being sent to the Pacific. It had been a long hard-fought series of battles back from the shellacking Americans took at Pearl Harbor. "I was an aviation electrician, a part of the ground crew maintenance, on several carriers while stationed in the British Solomon Islands, particularly at Henderson Field on Guadalcanal after the Marines had fought one of the bloodiest tasks of chasing the Japanese up into the hills.

"The taking of Guadalcanal was the first sign of hope of moving the Japanese north and returning the island to the British Solomon Islands. While I was on Guadalcanal, I witnessed some tremendous bloody sea battles in an effort to push Japan's fleet farther north. The Japanese flagship *Chokai* sank four unsuspecting American cruisers: the *Vincennes*, the *Quincy*, the *Astoria*, and the pride of the Australian Navy, the *Canberra*. During the night, all four were sunk, with the loss of one thousand lives.

"I was on Guadalcanal a year before I went back to the Fiji Islands, some sixty miles north, for some rest, recuperation, and treatment for my malaria. Most of the Marines and other military occupied Guadalcanal to some degree, then I made my way to the Russell Islands. I worked on bombers, dive-bombers, and PBYs.

"By August 1944, American forces had cleared the islands of Saipan, Tinian, and Guam in the Marianas. At Saipan, thirty-two thousand Japanese troops had fought to the death. Another twenty thousand civilians working on the island committed suicide before losing Saipan to the Allied forces. This victory gave the Americans control of Iwo Jima and Okinawa airbases for their B-29 bombers.

"*Enola Gay* and two other planes, packed with scientific equipment, flew over Hiroshima. Their code name 'Little Boy' dropped the first uranium bomb. Two-thirds of the city was destroyed in an instant. The Japanese would not relent until on August 9 another B-29, *Bocks Car*, took off from Tinian, carrying a plutonium type bomb, code-named 'Fat Man.' The industrial city of Nagasaki was the target by default.

"The weapons arsenal of Kokura was covered by a thick cloud cover and didn't serve as a suitable target. Just as many people died in Nagasaki as Hiroshima. The Soviet Union had declared war on Japan the previous day and invaded Manchuria. The fighting stopped on August 15, 1945.

"When I returned after two years in the Pacific, I was surprised that it was the women who were driving taxicabs, freight trucks, and ambulances. The war was the motivation to do something beyond their roles as stay-at-home wives and mothers to support the war effort. It was in Florida that I met Dorothy at a dance. Here was a young teacher and a WAVE third class from Idaho. I would like to think that she was soon smitten by this young Navy serviceman from Wyoming. Growing up during the Depression, I liked traveling, and I had military experiences. We found we had a lot in common.

Dorothy had a clearer understanding of what I had been through on Guadalcanal. That made it easier to make the transition back to coming home.

"We traveled by train on a fifteen-day furlough home to Idaho for our wedding in April 1945. Because it was wartime, Dot had to get special permission to wear a long white gown, as the military had to always wear her WAVE uniform in public. Dot was assigned to the Miami weather squadron for hurricane watching.

"Dorothy was discharged from the Navy when she became pregnant. I was assigned to work on the PBM seaplane. We lived in Banana River NAS where our two daughters were born. I was transferred often, and we lived in Guam, Japan, Adak, Alaska, California, Texas, Georgia, Virginia, Florida, and Washington. Dorothy taught the elementary grades in many of those states, including Oak Harbor."

After a thirty-year career, Casey retired in 1971 from NAS Whidbey as the ground electronics officer at AIMD (Aviation Intermediate Maintenance Department). The Baiers had an opportunity to do a lot of traveling before Dorothy made a commitment to sing in and direct many groups, including the choir at the Whidbey Presbyterian Church for eight years, and was a member of the Floyd Suther string ensemble. Her musical talents were a driving force in musicals at the Whidbey Playhouse.

"We have seen all fifty states, Canada and Mexico, a large portion of Europe and the Far East. We intended to return to New Zealand and Tasmania. We are still trying to talk Casey into going to the Antarctica, but he has put his foot down on that idea!" she said with a laugh. It pleases me to see the advances women have made worldwide, especially those in the military. I think we proved long ago that women are capable of doing just about anything! It is rewarding to know that I made my mark in history during World War II."

Dorothy Virginia Sheehan Baier passed away during this series of interviews. She is missed by her family and many friends. We'll remember her as an incredible and gifted woman.

Ray "John Wayne" Myers

Scouts and Raiders

As a youngster back in Kansas City, Missouri, John Wayne was his hero. Ray Myers's favorite pastime had been to go to the nickel theater Saturday mornings with his six-guns, no caps, buckled on his hips. John Wayne's faithful sidekicks in the theater seats could shoot at the "bad guys" until their trigger fingers were dog-tired. They could rest a bit while John was kissing the pretty girls.

"After the bombing of Pearl Harbor, young men traded in their youth to fight the Japanese or Hitler's Germany. Like John Wayne, they would shoot the bad guys and wish for pretty girls to kiss. After working in the Civilian Conservation Corps, I left for Great Lakes Naval Recruit Training Command. Next, it was Little Creek, Virginia, for training for the Landing Craft Infantry. Being trained to identify enemy aircraft was extremely boring for me. Besides, I couldn't stand the routine of standing, marching, or running in the mud and rain anymore. Being single, I volunteered for a secret program. We were loaded on a troop train with window blinds drawn. The train didn't stop until we reached a USO in Blue Field, West Virginia.

"Army and Navy personnel were assembled into two separate groups at the Amphibious Training Base at Fort Pierce, Florida, for seven and one-half months of training: to identify, reconnoiter an objective beach, maintain a position prior to a landing, and then guide the assaults in the water and on the beach. We were being trained as skilled Scouts and Raiders and Underwater Demolition Teams ('naked' warriors), which gave birth to the Navy SEALs.

"I learned the hard way that the term hadn't meant to be literally *naked*. The Atlantic Ocean tidelands are populated with treacherous stinging jellyfish. No women, just jellyfish. These jellyfish don't care what they grab on to as it swam by them. I came ashore with one of these jellyfish attached to everything I had that was a private part of my body. After four days and numerous bottles of calamine lotion, I finally got the swelling down. This narrative never fails to get laughs at Scouts and Raiders reunions.

"The Navy acquired the USS *Appalachian* (AGC-1) on 27 February 1943. Following the shakedown in the Chesapeake Bay, Capt. James M. Fernald transited the ship through the Panama Canal, north to San Diego, California, before heading for Hawaii. She was the first of three amphibian command ships. The *USS Blue Ridge* and *USS Rocky Mountain* followed in her wake. Each ship had six crews of six Scouts and Raiders plus their naval officers. Captain Fernald had the cool confidence of John Wayne around the top brass or in combat of the *USS Appalachian*. I liked him immediately.

USS *Appalachian* (AGC-1)

"Most of the photographers were filming from planes. Then their film plates were literally dropped off by hook and wire to the deck of the *USS Appalachian*. The negatives were rapidly developed in the ship's lab and presented to the brass in the War Command Room. I thought it looked like a plush hotel conference room. Twenty-four operators occupied the radio room adjacent to the War Command Room all hours a day. All incoming reports were on screens constantly, and then utilized to make command decisions.

"Among the brass on Captain Fernald's Amphibian Assault Command Ship were Rear Adm. Richard L. Connolly, Gen. Roy Stanley Geiger, USMC, who commanded the III Amphibious Corps, and a General Smith, who commanded the Army. They could call for whatever they considered necessary for an invasion: air strikes, aircraft carriers, troop convoys, absolutely anything that they needed for the assaults.

"As Captain Fernald's coxswain, I seldom performed the tasks for which I was trained. Once I piloted Captain Fernald's boat into a harbor with a seaplane ramp, I didn't make that error again. On the other side of the concrete seawall was a minefield. The ground was filled with white flags tied on wires. Rear Admiral Connolly may not have realized their purpose or was simply verifying what he thought they might be: a field of identified Japanese bombs that had not detonated on impact. 'Operation White Horse' was ordered. The brass wanted the minefield cleared and a bridge built across a ravine by 0400. During my midwatch, I listened to the radio chatter. By 0400, both tasks were completed.

Good view of village

Notice Pipe in belt

"These pictures were taken on a trip in search of Japanese in the Florida Islands. I was the coxswain in the scout boat from the *USS Appalachian*. The villagers were afraid of the Japanese and left their villages. The U.S. Navy had to prove that they were looking for Japanese soldiers still hiding in the jungle.

"I remember the day when Col. Carl Carlson, of the Marine Raiders, stood on the stern of the battleship *USS California*, giving the Special Forces orders: 'Take prisoners, they aren't trained in defensive interrogation.' I knew that those who could speak Japanese accompanied the Marines on the invasions. Any information obtained was radioed back to the command ship. On June she was hit by a shell from an enemy shore battery, which killed one man and wounded nine. Following Saipan, her heavy guns helped blast the way for the assault force in Guam and Tinian operations.

"The invasion of Roi and Namur Island in the northern part of the Kwajalein Atoll in the Marshall Islands was successful. Land-based planes from all three services and carrier aircraft piled blows with increased intensity upon the Marshall Islands. Underwater Demolition Teams met the challenge of disarming the teepee-like fortresses that stood sentry duty on the beaches. These 'naked warriors' wore only swimsuits, fins, and face masks on combat operations and saw action virtually on every island in the Pacific.

"As the Amphibian Assault and Invasion Command Ship, *Appalachian* remained on the perimeter of the battles. Taking possession of Saipan proved to be more difficult than the 'brass' had anticipated. Our tenacious troops on the beaches took the island inch by inch, killing thirty-two thousand Japanese. The casualties were high for our Marines too.

"On board the *Appalachian* was an operating room and surgeons, battle-weary Marines, with tears in their eyes, and a wounded buddy in their arms would plea for a corpsman or doctor to save the life of their trusted companion. But the IVs and bandages wouldn't be enough to save their lives. The dead were placed in wire baskets, and then arranged head to foot along the corridors of the ship. They were wrapped in mummy-like fashion until they could be taken ashore safely and buried.

"Any plans for taking Guam at this point had to be delayed. The *Appalachian* would have to return to Eniwetok and wait for more trained troops and assault equipment from Hawaii before the invasion of Guam. I saw things you don't want to see in the movies or read in the history books. My memories are filled with visions of the wounded, dying, amputated bodies and grotesque portions of human flesh of America's finest-fighting machines. I have no appropriate words to describe the carnage, the odors, and the sounds of death.

"Japanese prisoners of war had been interrogated, then removed from the area. What remained were bloody bloated bodies of the Japan's finest-fighting forces that had been bulldozed into craters formed by bombs dropped from the Japanese and American forces alike.

There was a painful silence. After a deep breath, Ray continued to clarify,"You see, many fathers back home wanted their sons send home a pair of Japanese ears to prove that they had been in the thick of the invasions. I was not one who could mutilate any body in such a manner to prove my bravery. I didn't pass judgment on those who did."

He pulled his own wallet out of his back pocket and paused before recounting the one occasion in which he found a dead body—a clean kill. Ray had intentions of taking a memento from the Jap's wallet to send home. Without a word, Ray flips open his own wallet to the pictures of his own family. He shakes his head, indicating that he couldn't do it by closing the wallet. Quietly Ray describes the color portrait of his enemy, his wife, and two small children; he knew that he couldn't take a man's most prized possession. For Ray's sensitive nature, just the memory is a deep scar.

"Burying the dead Japanese was an awful duty. I observed the process of mass burials into bomb-created craters. I won't forget the horrific cremations done by using massive flamethrowers.

"As a Scout and Raider, I made three invasions: Roi-Namur, Saipan, and Guam. On Eniwetok, I inspected the landing craft tanks (LCT) and Navy boats to make sure that their crews had properly maintained them. These boats were carrying food supplies and equipment back to the base. LCTs carried troops. After there was a rash of boats coming in need of repair, I discovered these boat crews were using old ammo and grenades for fishing. The ammunition flak was blowing holes in their own boats. Fishing season was officially *closed!*

"After a year on Eniwetok, as first-class boatswain mate, I was able to hitch a ride on a Coast Guard troopship headed for home. Etched in my memory was the dense indigo fog that swallowed the ship somewhere near San Francisco Bay at 0400.

"Cheering broke out below from the mess hall, and soon all ambulatory Navy personnel of every rank were dancing in celebration on all decks. A young crewman had just won an all-night crap game. A mound of $1, $5, $10, $20, and a few $50 bills, the size of a bushel basket, was being swept up by the winner and stuffed into every cavity of his uniform. Abruptly the speaker system blared out, "Now hear this! Now hear this! Japan has asked for a cease-fire!" Those

who slept through the announcement were dragged out of their bunks, swearing that it was a horrible joke, while others made their way to the top deck just in time to see the fog part like velvet curtains, and the Golden Gate Bridge appeared to welcome our men home from the Pacific.

"The next bus transported this 'John Wayne' back to my home in Kansas City, Missouri, where I worked as a civilian until I reenlisted in 1957. I retired in Oak Harbor, Washington, as one of our nation's first Navy Seals.

Donald Gordon

Bonsai Charge, a Baptism by Fire on Sulphur Island

Born and raised in the San Francisco Bay area of California at the age of twenty-one, Don Gordon entered college with an artistic aptitude, with an emphasis on sculpture and pottery. He loved working with his hands. Don also had always been interested in flying. As a youngster, he had a passion for building models of various planes, and he could identify them all. He wanted to fly! The U.S. Army Air Corps was only interested in experienced and trained pilots until the war in the Pacific Theater heated up, and they needed to recruit replacement pilots regardless of their age.

His older brother Jack, a cavalryman at heart, was an observer in the tank corps in the European Theater. He survived action in North Africa and served under General Patton in France. (Ironically, he, too, was killed in a jeep accident, like General Patton before coming home, after the war ended in Europe.]

For Don to get into the Army Air Cadet Training program, he would have to leave his wife and a young son in California. He had been waiting and preparing for this opportunity to fly for his country. Don received his pilot's training at King City, California; Lancaster, California; and Luke Field, in Arizona. Luke Field had various 'Texan' trainer planes: the Navy SNJs, the Army Air Corps AT-6s, and the 'Recruit,' PT-22, which were used by both Navy and Army pilots. Officially, Don was in the VII Fighter Command, the only fighter group attached to the Twentieth Army Air Corps and Twenty-first Fighter Group B-29s.

Don met the new sweetheart in his life, a P-51 number 205 with extended fuel tanks. Her name was *Miss Behavin'*. Her squadron colors were blue on the tips of her nose, wings, and tail rudder. All the squadron-colored markings were edged with black. *Miss Behavin'* was painted on her nose. In January 1945, twenty-nine newly trained fighter pilots assigned to the Forty-sixth Fighter Squadron left Luke Field and headed for two months of combat training at Mokelai, Hawaii. Pilots on leave met with other pilots flying P-38s and P-39s.

"I was to get at least ten hours of training in the P-51. However, it was more like four hours before we headed for Iwo Jima. Because of a tragic mishap when a Navy bomber had taken off by accident in the middle of six hundred fighter planes. The various planes had been arranged in lined formations, which was great for inspections. After the incident, the Navy had to shove the burning planes off the island and into the ocean with a bulldozer. [We laid out our planes separately during training and in arrangements in order to avoid a complete strafing of our aircraft by the Japanese.] The Navy was thrilled to see the Army Air Corps come flying onto Iwo Jima, the island of sulphur.

"Everyone in the Twenty-first Fighter Group's complement of beautiful new P-51 Mustangs was anxious for their first mission when we finally arrived at Iwo Jima. The Marines had done their job by taking the island of Iwo Jima at a very high cost. They were packing up to leave, and the Army was expected to hold the island. As real estate, the island was worthless. However, holding it meant a step closer to Tokyo. Our job was to protect the B-29 bombers flying loaded from Iwo Jima to Japan.

"The original plan was to take Iwo Jima in three or four days and then to proceed up Chichi Jima and take that island. Our group was scheduled to move to Chichi Jima when it was secured. The Twenty-first Fighter Group was living in Army tents on the west side parallel to the Chidori Airfield, airfield number 2, where our P-51s were tied down and a half mile from the former enemy lines. It was boring just waiting around for orders to finally get a chance for action over the home islands of Japan. Fishing from the rocky shoreline proved uneventful. The extensive bombing prior to the invasion either had chased off all of the fish or had killed a majority of them.

"Herb Bowden and I decided life here was dull on Iwo Jima after a couple days. We decided to hike down the island to watch the fighting. We were young, naive, and totally unaware of the possible danger that awaited us. To avoid the marine guard who would just send us back, we left the road and traversed the rough ground, unaware that we were traveling across a minefield. The area had not been cleared of land mines, and we were fortunate not to locate one by accident.

"We hiked north until we saw a group of caves on our right, which looked like it might be of interest. We found a large unexploded U.S. naval shell had been dropped into one of them. The shell was about a foot and a half in diameter and perhaps six or seven feet in length. We both slid down the shell and went into a cave. Inside, we were disappointed to find only first aid supplies, but no souvenirs.

"Resuming our hike, we located another cave a short distance away. Following a tunnel down into the ground, we went down the chiseled-out steps to a secluded room below ground level. Adjoining rooms and another staircase lead farther down into the ground. Using flashlights for illumination, we suddenly heard some noises that we could not identify and assumed they were the enemy. So both of us ran hurriedly up the steps and left the cave.

"We hiked the last couple of miles toward the north end of the island and heard gunfire coming from the beach below, settling down on the edge of the embankment and watching as well as we could 'the final taking of Iwo Jima.' Bullets ricocheted off the rocks nearby, but we were not overly concerned. When they increased appreciably, we quickly decided that we had better 'get the hell out of there.' When we stood up to leave, the number of ricocheting bullets suddenly increased. It finally dawned upon us that *we* were the targets of gunfire from the Japanese some distance away.

"We dashed back down the trail from which we had just come and ran between tall rain-washed hillocks, perhaps fifteen feet high and very steep. Beinging in great shape, we ran approximately seven miles back to where the same marine was still standing on duty. Avoiding him, we made our way back to our group campsite located only a half mile south of the enemy lines. Meeting a group of Marines on their way back to their own encampment just south of ours, we stopped in to share a few cans of beer. Herb and I told them about the caves and the shooting.

"With sober faces, they informed us that even the Marines would not go where we had gone with anything less than a full platoon of armed soldiers. They said we had bypassed at least 2,500 Japanese in caves during their efforts to re-secure the island. They made it very clear that we were lucky to come out of no-man's-land alive. They also informed us the Marines were leaving Iwo Jima the next day. The Army planned to disembark from the ships in the harbor and maintain control of Iwo Jima under the leadership of General Moore.

"That evening, both Herb and I were rather reflective and quiet. I settled down in my luxurious pad and made myself as comfortable as possible. I had laid an air mattress under my sleeping bag and a small throw rug to keep my feet off the black sand of the island. An old orange crate at the head of my bed supported my alarm clock, gas mask, and my .45 Colt revolver. I thought I had a rather cozy setup. It was still dark when we were awakened by loud explosions. The first thought that came to my mind was that the Marines were celebrating by exploding hand grenades, and I tried to settle back waiting for sunrise. The explosions continued, and some sounded too close for comfort."

Military records verify that during the early hours, the Japanese soldiers attacked elements of the Twenty-first Fighter Group of the U.S. Army Air Corps in their encampment. Assisted by a few Marines, the Twenty-first fighter pilots made a counterattack in tent-to-tent combat. They killed approximately 250 of the enemy. Twenty of the group personnel were reported killed, and fifty, including Twenty-first FG commander Colonel Kenneth Powell, were wounded.

If Lt. Don Gordon had not reacted aggressively, with an instinct for survival, and not shown leadership during that early-morning attack, the last mass suicidal attack by the Japanese may have succeeded. Then history of the war on Iwo Jima may have been written differently.

"I remember the early morning of March 26, 1945. Whether it was the escapade Herb and I had pulled the previous afternoon in exploring the enemies' concrete fortifications or the sounds or the continuous explosions too close for comfort, I couldn't sleep. Looking up at the top of the tent, I could see tiny holes had suddenly appeared. They were machine gun bullet holes. I rolled out of the sack and on to the tarp. I put on my pants and boots in a horizontal position faster than I had ever put them on before! After alerting others in the tent, they were wrestling with their clothes while choking on their fear.

"I heard a friend of mine cry out, I ran out of our tent to the one behind us. One of the pilots in there was bleeding badly from a head wound. Oblivious to what was actually happening, I told him I would find the medic. I ran down the back row of tents until I reached 'Doc's' tent. I called out for him as I stuck my head in. I was quickly grabbed and pulled inside with guns pointed directly at me. The pilots informed me that we were under attack by the Japanese, some in the uniforms of dead Marines. Therefore, I couldn't leave their tent.

"I was insistent that I needed to return with help for my friend. The medic pulled my arm and said, 'Shut up! Let's go!' Crawling out under the tent flap and into the next tent, we found two badly wounded pilots slashed with knives. Dragging them to a shallow foxhole in the corner of the tent, the medic went for more help. Then, I realized I had left my Colt .45 on the orange crate by my cot. The only weapon I had was my knife. Soon three of us were huddling together shivering with fear as grenades hit the top of the tents and rolled down the side exploding only a few feet from our refuge.

"It was fortunate that the foxhole had been dug at the corner of the tent because the grenades rolled away from the tents. Near the inside corner of the tent behind me appeared a shadowy shape. I looked up cautiously during the stillness and saw a man standing up in the tent going through some clothes. I yelled at him to get down when suddenly the impact of gunfire knocked him out. He had been a Japanese soldier going through clothes looking for souvenirs.

"Word was passed that we were all to scramble for safety into the garbage pit behind the mess tent. I sent the two wounded pilots ahead and then bolted out of the foxhole, darting left and right to avoid being hit by stray gunfire. 'I had seen this in a movie and thought it was the way to avoid being hit.' I hit the ground six or eight feet from the mess tent. A strange bicycle leaned against it. I was getting ready to get up and make another dash for the pit when I looked in the direction of the commanding officer's tent.

"I saw someone run out and jump into a barrel that had been dug into the ground as a foxhole. Then I saw another figure dash out of the tent and leap for the barrel just as a black object arched toward its target. The object hit the second figure on the chest, and it exploded. His head went straight into the air, and his hand landed in the spokes of the bicycle next to where I lay. Fueled on adrenaline,

I got up and ran around the tent, diving into the garbage pit with other pilots and ground crew huddled together.

"I continued running to where the Marines' compound was located and get some help. I found a foxhole with a tent over it and asked the two Marines to come and help us. They declined stating that they were scheduled to go home in just a few hours, and they couldn't risk it. I asked for grenades and carbines and was told to take the 'Jap truck' to the ordinance depot and get what I needed there. I started the truck, but it had so many gears I could not get it to move in any direction except backward.

"Thank God our executive officer drove up in a jeep containing several boxes of grenades. It didn't take us long to unload the heavy crates and break them open. I stuffed as many grenades that would fit in the front of my shirt and in my pockets. We crawled on our bellies between the tents looking for any of our men that were still alive. As we crawled to the last row of tents, we could see the concrete gun emplacements where the Japanese soldiers could fire their rifles into our tents. Obviously, they did not spot us, or we would have been dead.

"I rolled over on to my back, pulled out a grenade, and pulled the pin. Fearful that the weight of it might cause me to drop it, I held it close like a letter from home. I threw that grenade straight and through into the gun emplacement. Japanese soldiers attempted to climb out of their refuge. Then they rolled back in after the grenade had exploded. I made several other direct hits into the emplacemen when other pilots crawled up and began firing their carbines at the Japanese soldiers as they rolled out of the safety of another gun emplacement.

"The firing finally settled down enough that I could hear a marine in a poncho yelling at us, 'Get up off your asses and fight like men!' Unable to convince us, he turned away as a tank pulled up, began firing into the gun emplacement and the shallow foxhole nearby. Suddenly, this brave marine sergeant slumped into the ground with a bullet hole in his head.

"As I crawled down the last row of tents looking for survivors, I saw a Japanese soldier tap his helmet with his grenade (a suicidal gesture) and held it to his chest. Why he didn't just throw the grenade is a question I couldn't answer then, nor can I now. He died without his head.

"I pulled open a tent flap, I saw one of our pilots lying on his stomach and partially buried in the black sand appearing to have been shot. I put my hand on his leg to see if he was still alive. He jumped, not knowing that it was me who was there. By this time, the fighting for tonight was over. The man I had rescued was a pilot named Felix whom I knew well. We all collected again in the garbage pit, waiting for orders. The horror of the last three or four hours had crawled into our senses like weevils. We could not cut them out of our mind's eye or from our thoughts.

"Sandwiches were handed out. To lighten the atmosphere and always the joker, I took a sandwich apart and put a clean bandage on the Spam inside. Then I put catsup and mayonnaise on it and put the top back on and rewrapped it. It was not long until another pilot picked it up and took a big bite out of it. The bandage pulled out and flopped onto his chin. He quickly pulled it out of his mouth and threw it up into the air. Others around me were in on the joke, and laughter broke the silence. It was perhaps a cruel joke, but it did help break the silent despair in all who were fortunate enough to witness.

"Lt. Harry Martin, of the Fifth Pioneer Battalion, who had organized a hasty defense line, rushed into the fight to rescue wounded men and launched a rapid attack. Killed in action, Lieutenant Martin would be the first pilot in the Twenty-first Fighter Group to win the Medal of Honor. By morning, I estimated forty-four pilots were killed, another eighty-eight attempted to regain the island of Iwo Jima were injured, nine Marines killed, another thirty-one wounded. This was Japan's last organized attempt to regain control of Iwo Jima.

The 21st Fighter Group's officer's area was the center of the fighting when Japanese soldiers slipped through the lines and launched an early morning attack on the camps near airfield number two. Interestingly, the angular shape of the tents tended to shed the grenades thrown into the area and lessen their effectiveness. (U.S. Army Air Forces via National Archives)

This group of tents, which was somewhat isolated from the rest of the camp, was raised by the newly arrived Twenty-first Fighter Group pilots.

This choice of tent location made them more vulnerable to attack by the desperate Japanese soldiers. Others had previously dug deep foxholes into the black sulfuric sand. They weren't taking any chances. This battle proved to be the beginning of the end of the Japanese-organized resistance. The fighting continued until the end of May.

"Later in my tent, I found my buddy Herb Bowden face own on my cot. Herb had been killed with a bullet just below his nose. My cot was a mess! My gas mask on the second shelf was riddled with holes, but the alarm clock on the top of the crate was miraculously intact. I tried later to mend the holes in my air mattress but gave up after patching twenty-three of them. A new cot, mattress, and sleeping bag were issued to me.

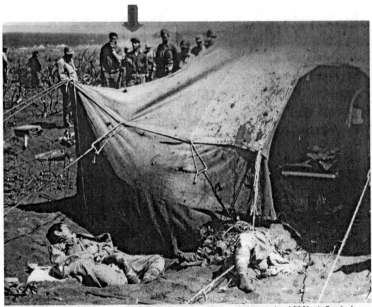

Men come to look at the carnage surrounding the 21st officer's tents on the late morning of 26 March. Two dead Japanese soldiers lie just outside this tent's entrance. Another enemy fighter was killed just inside the doorway. His body can barely be seen in the shadows on the floor of the tent. (U.S. Army Air Forces via National Archives)

[The tents have been identified by Capt. Don Gordon himself. This particular tent was his and identified in the publication 'Strike and Return: American Air Power and the Fight for Iwo Jima'" By Cory Graff, with his permission. Don is standing under the arrow as identified on March 16, 2009.]

The first long-range aerial mission of the Twenty-first Fighter Group against the mainland of Japan began on April 7, 1945, and like Don, most of the young pilots were anticipating their first combat mission. A few were disappointed. As for Don, he shot down one enemy and assisted with bringing down another. This mission marked the first-time fighters had escorted bombers over Japan. The Twenty-first would escort B-29 bombers over enemy airfields, industrial targets, and would engage rival Japanese fighter aircraft.

When asked if he ever saw the faces of the enemy fighter pilots, he said yes. "Once I had been wingtip to wingtip, and we saluted one another. Then I outmaneuvered him in my P-51 and shot him in the wings. The pilot somersaulted out of his cockpit and parachuted down into the sea."

When asked if he then shot the parachuting pilot, he said, "Oh no, it was a matter of respect and honor." At one point, Don had tallied sixteen successful kills and twelve probable kills. When the Japanese no longer came after the B-29s, the fighters went in hot pursuit after them whenever possible.

Don and his P-51, *Miss Behavin'*, were photographed on several occasions and had the opportunity to do a few rollover maneuvers for the movie cameras.

[Japanese aircraft suicide crashes on Iwo Jima, National Archives]

Miss Behavin' photographed well. He flew her with pride on seventeen (very long range) combat missions, racking up more than two thousand miles, ten hours' flight plus one to two hours of combat with Japanese fighter planes until mid-August of 1945. This meant approximately twelve to fourteen hours in the saddle. These flights, although dangerous, were nothing like the combat he faced his second day on Iwo Jima. Don is very modest about just how courageous he was during the *banzai attack* on the Twenty-first Fighter Group pilots. He turned down the Silver Star because he felt that he only did what he was supposed to do. His only regret is that he wasn't able to save more of his fellow pilots. For those whose lives he saved, Lt. Don Gordon is a true hero! Of the twenty-nine pilots who flew overseas with Don to Iwo Jima, only three pilots returned to the States.

"P-51 fighter pilots had the responsibility of protecting and guiding B-29 pilot and crews on bombing missions to Japan. Upon returning from one of those missions, I received orders to locate and rescue Lt. Joseph Coons under cloudy conditions a few miles off the coast of Japan. The rest on the 121 aircraft assigned bombing mission continued flying above the cloud cover at twelve-thousand-foot elevation. Once I located Lieutenant Coons, he was flying at approximately an elevation of seven thousand feet. I gave him order to bail out. Apparently, Lieutenant Coons couldn't hear me on his radio, so I tapped his wing at four thousand feet. This was the definitive signal to *bail out now!* But Lieutenant Coons's plane continued to plummet to four hundred feet before he prepared to bail out. I watched as Lieutenant Coons bail out, hitting his foot on the aircraft's rudder.

"The wind pulled the pilot on his face, dragging Lieutenant Coons along the surface of the water. I made several attempts to cut his parachute lines with my propeller blades. I was unsuccessful, and Lieutenant Coons was being dragged out of sight below the surface of the ocean. He never came to the surface. I was now flying somewhere between the cloud cover and the ocean. The clouds were so thick I could only see about three feet in front of me. The other planes flying above the cloud cover at twelve thousand feet had no chance of safely landing on Iwo Jima, an island about 7.5 miles long and 0.5 miles wide. I had no choice but to remain flying at number 187, a code key for 187-degree straight south.

"My compass wasn't terribly reliable. I was isolated from my wingman and on my own. When I radioed for assistance, some general bellowed back, 'Look it up on the f*******map!' At this point, I figured I was about ten miles from Japan and eight hundred miles from Iwo Jima. I turned the radio off for a couple hours. When I flew over Chichi Jima, I knew that I was three hundred miles north of Iwo Jima. I spotted a U.S. naval destroyer. I tried to radio them, but they never answered. I tipped my wing to let them know that I was having some trouble. Instead, I got four shots off my left wing—so much for bailing out and being rescued. They must have been chasing an enemy prey.

"I stayed close the surface of the water until there was a momentary break in the clouds. Directly in front of me was Kita Iwo, a high pinnacle-shaped island approximately forty miles north of Iwo Jima. 'Pork chops' code came in from radio control on Iwo Jima. Until then, I was still flying blind, as were the 120 planes above the cloud cover. Radio control told us to watch for the clear spot on the open edge at the north end of Iwo. As soon as I spotted it, I recognized my crew chief banging his red cap with joy. I landed first and hit the runway. The other 120 planes landed behind me, just as if it were planned."

Don is the only survivor to date living with these grim memories. Returning to his home in California, Don resumed his education for a career in teaching. Don taught Art in Richmond, California, for thirty-nine years before retiring. He and his wife visited his son up here in the Northwest and decided to move to Whidbey Island. Don has a few samples of his pottery and a beautiful colored pen-and-ink drawing in his apartment. He is clearly a man of honor, intelligence, and artistic talent. Because of men like Capt. Don Gordon, our country is truly blessed. As for Don, he often wonders just where the Air Corps pilots, his buddies, and his dear wife will be waiting for him. "Dear God, let it be heaven, we've already been through hell."

Leon "Lee" Sher

Japan Via Iwo Jima

When we think of Iwo Jima, most of us think of all the Marines that gave their lives to raise the American flag on a Japanese territory that had not been invaded for more than four thousand years. Twenty-one thousand Japanese soldiers defended Iwo Jima; it was their unsinkable carrier. The volcanic-ash-covered Sulphur Island was fortified with concrete bunkers and gun emplacements. Underneath the scrub, ash-like soil and volcanic rock was a maze of tunnels by which they could hide and defend their prized possession.

The Fifth Marines landed on the south end of the island, but they were not prepared for the black glassy, sandy conditions of the terrain. Thirty thousand of U.S. troops landed, and 2,400 were hit by accurate Japanese firepower. After gaining control of 4,000 yards of the beachhead, they moved inland and took control of airfield number 1. The Fourth Marines fought their way up the east coast and the Third held the center of the island. The combat and carnage continued for another three months, and 30 percent of the landing forces were lost.

Second Lt. Lee Sher, a former member of the Forty-seventh Fighter Squadron, Fifteenth Fighter Group, and Seventh Army Force, as a P-51 pilot, has nothing but words of praise for these brave men. Lee Sher was one of the fighter pilots that escorted B-29s from the airbase on Iwo Jima on bombing missions to Japan. One of the more horrific accounts recorded is the night when Japanese soldiers, wearing the U.S. Marine uniforms came onto airfield number 2. They bayoneted sleeping pilots, killing twenty-four of twenty-seven of the Forty-sixth Fighter Squadron, Twenty-first Fighter Group, during this daring suicide mission. Days and nights were filled with terror for exhausted Marines. Foxholes were almost impossible to dig. The Japanese knew every inch of the island. They would crawl on their bellies through island fortifications to kill isolated Marines, and disappear again in an underground cavern or tunnel.

Gone were the days of Lee's youth back in San Francisco and Oakland, California. After graduation from Fremont High School in Oakland in 1942, Lee got a job working at Moore Shipyard in Alameda. Because of his mechanical drawing background, Lee soon had a job drawing keel plates of C-2 cargo vessels as a junior draftsman at age seventeen. He had always been interested in building model airplanes, and in his earlier years he had ridden his bicycle down to Oakland Airport and washed airplanes for $0.75 an hour for the Gilmore Air Service. Sometimes the pilots took Lee up for short check rides, and he was hooked on flying from being a passenger in a Ford Tri-Motor and other vintage transport planes from the 1930s.

Going to college during the week, and working on the weekends, Lee passed the exams for the aviation cadet and signed up with the reserves. On February 7, 1943, Lee was called up to active duty. He went to the University of Nevada-Reno for one semester as part of his aviation cadet training. They got ten hours of light aircraft training at the Reno Sky Ranch. He had additional flight training at Thunderbird Field near Phoenix, Arizona; basic at Pecos, Texas; and advanced training at Luke Field outside of Phoenix. On March 11, 1944, Lee became a second lieutenant, and in twenty days, he was shipped to Hawaii.

During his career as a pilot, Lee flew twenty-nine varieties of aircraft. On Iwo Jima, Lee flew long-range missions, escorting B-29 bombers. In a single mission, he spent eight to eleven hours in the P-51 Mustang. "The aircraft was an extension of the pilot, like an equestrian on his horse. A fighter pilot had to learn how to survive on split-second decisions, instinct, and wit, with self-confidence that bordered on arrogance. The only person you completely trusted was yourself, thus we had a reputation for being a lone wolf or a hotshot," said Lee.

[In this permission photo of the Forty-seventh Fighter Squadron, Lee is the third pilot in the first row on the left.]

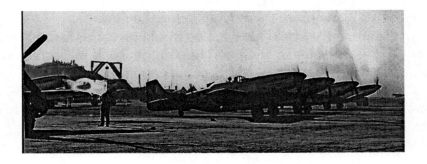

[P-51 Fighters planes on Iwo Jima]

All pilots had learned to shoot first upon takeoff from the tarmac, knowing that the Japanese would be waiting to shoot at the coolant or the prop on the single-engine fighter planes and external fuel tanks. The fighter pilots, like Lee, learned to be independent, think fast, and respond instantaneously.

A pilot and his plane are one and the same. One time, Lee knew immediately that something was wrong, so he cut the engine. Lee leaped out of the cockpit, tucked in his elbows tight against his body, and rolled off the wing. His plane took a nosedive down onto the two external gas tanks and came to a screeching halt. Lee ran toward the edge of the airfield. Dazed and still in shock, Lee found himself in a foxhole with a big burly marine when the gas tanks in his plane blew.

"Hey, you can't stay in here!" the marine bellowed. Still in shock, Lee started to climb out as he'd been ordered. But just as quickly, he was grabbed from behind and yanked back into the hole. "Well, you'd better stay here for a while."

After waiting in the foxhole with the marine for a while, Lee got up and walked up the strip behind the chaplain who's looking at the plane crash. When Lee tapped him on the shoulder, the chaplain jumped and turned around. His face blanched when he saw that Lee was all there. Seeing that he had survived the crash, the chaplain casually said, "Darn, I just wasted a perfectly good sermon."

When Lee had the opportunity to examine the remainder of his plane, he found that the rudder only had one of three required universal hinges attached to the tail. Apparently, the mechanic on duty had forgotten to secure the other two hinges. Lee could have filed a complaint, but he didn't. He understood that the young mechanic had been on duty for thirty-six hours straight. From then on, Lee checked his plane more thoroughly before he flew.

[As serendipity would have it, Lee would meet this same Marine thirty-five years later in their condominiums back in Sacramento, California. Their families would become good friends.]

On a mission from Iwo Jima to Japan, Lee was flying "tail-end Charlie" when a Tojo with four 20 mm cannons came out of nowhere. The leader of the four P-51s scissored too quickly, leaving Lee vulnerable. He took two 20 mm shots in the right wing, one through the roof on his canopy, and the fourth in the left wing. Armed with instinct and intelligence, Lee dove out of it then limped back home. Without an airfoil, he literally broke the plane in a crash landing. He walked away, suffering only a bruised nose from hitting his face on the gun sight.

Ironically, at the end of the war, Lee received a bill from the U.S. government for the "missing" plane for $51,389.14. Lee had been checked out on the plane while stationed on Iwo Jima and had not returned it. The form 1-A had not been returned either that would have explained the crash on the runway that nearly cost Lee his life.

Lee attributes his survival to his small build, 90 percent training, and 10 percent instinct for having flown nineteen successful missions between Japan and Iwo Jima. His most infamous flight was the one in which he was returning from one of those missions from Osaka. Lee calls it stupidity or just dumb luck, but he took a scenic detour and spotted an unfamiliar ship anchored in a cove. He thought it was an Army transport. As he flew closer, he could see that the ship was

taking on ammunition and gunpowder. When he got closer, Lee could see that below him in the fjord was a Japanese destroyer with 20 and 40 mm antiaircraft guns. Flying at the speed of more that 400 mph, wielding six .50 caliber guns, he opened fire on the enemy destroyer. He had shot enemy aircraft, trains, and troop carriers before—now he was blazing bullets across the hull of a Japanese destroyer. Lee was so close that he could see the shine of a sailor's belt buckle and the fear on his face. His tracer bullets hit the trail of loose gunpowder on the deck, which ignited the first detonation in the forward Castile. It was the fuse to a series of explosions that sank the Japanese destroyer.

A gun camera provided proof of Lee's expertise as a P-51 pilot. After the war, *Time-Life* magazine bought and published his pictures. For these successes, First Lt. Lee Sher received the Silver Star for Gallantry in Action, the Distinguished Flying Cross, and Air Medal with four clusters, a Presidential Citation, and the usual operational ribbons. Shortly after the war ended on August 15, 1945, he returned in September to San Francisco. Per his promise to his mother, he returned to college and joined the reserves.

In January of 1948, he was recalled to active duty until February of 1950. When the Korean War broke out in July of 1950, he was recalled again and served until October of 1952. He resigned his commission as a captain to spend more time with his family and to continue his education. Lee Sher, an older, a more modest and wiser fighter pilot, came to appreciate all branches of the military, especially those Marines who contributed so much to end the war in the Pacific.

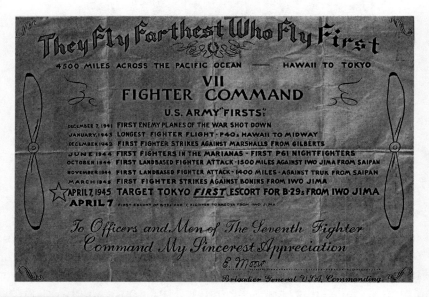

Captain Lee Sher retired here in Oak Harbor, taught business and finance at Skagit Valley College. He enjoys the company of other WWII veterans around the pool table at the senior center when he's not traveling.

Laurin "Bud" Zylstra

Ninth Engineering Command Build, Defend, Maintain

Oak Harbor has always been home to Laurin "Bud" Zylstra. Bud graduated from Oak Harbor High School in June of 1941 and started working on construction. The first job was unloading lumber from a barge until he got a job building "Victory Homes." They made up for lost time when lumber was available. Bud and his crew, with their individual trade skills, could build a complete home in one day!

"My brother Donald had been working at the shipyard in Bremerton, Washington, and had been deferred twice before the Navy put him to work on a salvage ship as a machinist. Don was stationed aboard an ocean-going tugboat to Shanghai; there he happened to meet the

daughter of our church pastor, Vander Woede. She was a nurse there, and it was quite a surprise for both of them. Don returned to Long Beach Island, California, until his ship was decommissioned.

"Soon to be drafted, I decided to enlist. My vision test scores didn't meet Navy standards, but I found a window of opportunity or the Army found it for me. Twenty-four boarded the bus with me and headed for Fort Lewis, Washington. Then I went on to Jefferson Barracks near St. Louis, Missouri, for basic training. After going on to Camouflage School at Fort Belvoir, Virginia, I received orders to report to Richmond, Virginia, because of my mechanical drafting and drawing experiences. The new 926th Engineer Aviation Regiment (926 EAR) was formed and connected to the Eighth Army Air Corps. This unique Regimental Headquarters combined personnel ranging in rank from private first class to colonel (Col. Eric Dougan) and included draftsmen, engineers, equipment operators, motor pool, and medical divisions.

"Late August 1943, as Private First Class Zylstra, I had waited for days before I sailed for England on the *Queen Elizabeth*. It only took five days for the crossing. I rotated sleeping one night on the deck and the next in a bunk. The ship arrived in the outside channel into the Firth (inlet) of the Clyde. The dock couldn't handle a ship the size of the *Queen Elizabeth*, so we departed the ship near Glasgow, Scotland, using tenders that had to go back and forth to unload the twelve thousand GIs. Before we boarded a train to Bury St. Edmunds, England, the GIs were served a canteen cup of tea and cookies.

"There, the other engineers and I were given drafting tables and we set to work providing the necessary designs for aircraft landing strips for the Allied aircraft. Plans and drawings formulated what equipment would be needed to reconstruct the airfields that had been destroyed by the German bombs. After seven months of repairing and building airfields, we moved closer to the location from which we would cross the English Channel onto Normandy. While we were at this staging area near South Hampton England, the engineering unit of the Eighth Army Group officially became the Ninth Engineering Command Regiment connected with the Ninth Army Air Corps.

"The airstrips in England needed constant reassessment due to the moist climate. A tar paper layer (dubbed "stamp licker") was applied to the compacted gravel, square mesh, and sod. These fields were okay for lighter aircraft. When steel planks were used, they occasionally buckled or rolled up underneath the aircraft's landing gear, it was catastrophic. We also prepared the heavy earth-moving equipment, bulldozers, and graders to be seaworthy for crossing the channel and ready to keep on going after they hit the beach at Normandy.

"I often used official Army photos to determine the conditions suitable for aircraft operations. Studies from aerial photographs helped the engineers to determine the locations of preferred dry-weather earth and stable soil conditions in France. The aerial photos of potential sites were taken and viewed in sequence. The lenses they used gave the objects the appearance of having three dimensions. The Engineering Aviation Regiment and Headquarters then made their decisions regarding the procedures for clearing, grading, sprinkling, drainage, and the compacting to be performed by the four battalions that worked under Engineering Aviation Regiment. As Regimental Headquarters and the Headquarters Company, they had the responsibility to provide equipment to all divisions as needed.

"German photo-reconnaissance noted the physical arrangements of the Allied troop tents, barracks, and equipment. I recall a specific strike made by the Germans, who had determined the 'heart of every tent' by the infrared glow of the stoves. Using the photos and flares to target what they perceived to be industrial buildings and headquarters, because of the tents' stove stacks and heat patterns. The troops heard the whistle of the bombs before they hit. Soil and debris from one of the explosions rained on the tents during that night. A routine that wasn't new to them.

"The next morning, I was in the mess tent eating when the flap flew open wide enough for me to see a group of men behind their tent studying a mound of dirt. Curious, my tent mates and I joined our officers. We found ourselves standing on the brink of a crater more than fifty feet in diameter and a twelve-foot-deep center pit. Our tent had been in that location the day before. Just hours before the bombing, we had moved our tent up onto a slope because of water in the corner of our tent. That was the closest call I would experience personally. I felt, the Good Lord was looking over me. And this was a reminder to me that the Lord would send me home."

However, the danger increased for others as D-day (June 6, 1944) approached. Every division and unit worked its way toward Southampton, the English Channel, and ultimately, Normandy, France. The subsequent construction of airfields in France would be the primary responsibility of the Ninth Engineer Command. The Engineering Aviation Regiment, including Bud, crossed the channel during the night of June 27 on a Canadian ship, the *Prince Henry*. They landed on Utah Beach approximately ten miles from Mont St. Michel near the junction between Cherbourg and Breast Peninsula. Their immediate task was to repair and reconstruct the airfields that the Allied forces had previously bombed. Now they needed to be leveled so that the Army Air Corps could land in the American section of France for fuel or repairs.

"We came ashore in the sector known to Americans as Utah Beach. As mentioned before, our task was, with our engineering skills, to determine the most efficient way to tear down airfields that could be utilized by the Germans, and repair, rebuild, or construct new airfields that would facilitate the liberation of France and General George S. Patton's troop movement from Carentan, Alencon, Paris and detour at the Battle of the Bulge."

In France, photo-reconnaissance, aerial maps, and intelligence reports continually helped provide a preliminary physical layout of the construction needed for the next airfield. Engineers determined the direction of the runways, orientation, and appropriate construction materials and the availability of natural materials. The Engineering Aviation Regiment was to follow in the wake of General George S. Patton's Army and turned sod into airfields as efficiently as possible.

"Wintering in Saint Nicolas, we were completely bogged down at Nancy-Essey until March 20. The Ninth Engineering Command pushed on over the Rhine, Lorsch, and Furth, building, defending, and maintaining the airfields that kept our bombers flying over Germany. As quickly as one airfield was repaired or constructed, it was immediately occupied. In a mere forty days after the invasions, our regiment planned the occupation of airfields for fifty-eight squadrons from Normandy, France, to Nuremburg, Germany.

This trailer, like Col. Dougan's, was made from wrecked gliders by this crew.

"General Patton was sweeping across France faster than the fuel and supply lines could keep up. He was determined to lead his Third Army right into the heart of Germany. Closer to the supply lines, the 926th Engineer Aviation Regiment engineers and draftsmen built or reconstructed airfields in England and France totaling more than three hundred in their wake before the war ended.

"While in France, I passed through Luneville, spotting my cousin Wes Zylstra from the command car with Lieutenant Konert to locate the possible airfield. I yelled to Wes that I would be coming back. It was a long two weeks before I returned. Wes had been on a reconnaissance mission and was now up at the front line. I got permission from the Thirty-Sixth Headquarters to ride in an ambulance up to Wes's location. There the two of us met and spent the night reminiscing.

"During that night near Bischwiller, the Germans had blown up the dike that washed out the two-lane road and the valley between the front line and headquarters. By the time I had returned by ambulance, I had missed my ride back to my own unit and had no pass to justify my presence at Luneville. Stranded and without orders, I was considered AWOL from my unit. I was thrown in the guardhouse without the privilege of calling my unit.

"After spending a night in the 'hoosegow,' the guard finally honored my request for paper and pencil. I wrote a letter to the sergeant of the guard requesting that he call my company,

giving him the number of my outfit and a request for someone to come and pick me up in the company jeep. Fortunately, all was forgiven and my record was cleansed, my 'Good Conduct' record was still intact.

"When the curtains fell on the 'European Theater' in April of 1945, I had been officially transferred to the Thirty-third Photoreconnaissance Squadron. The rest of Ninth Engineering Command moved in to Strasburg, Germany, on April 6, 1945; Mannheim, Germany, April 10; and Nuremberg, April 24. We thought it was very thoughtful of the Germans to leave this luxurious swimming pool for the GIs out in the hot sun. I have to admit that I was caught on camera enjoying myself. This vacation didn't last long because of the point system that worked to my advantage, I was sent home on a troop ship back to Boston, Massachusetts.

"Most of my outfit stayed in Europe for the Army of Occupation of Europe. I went aboard a C-47 after a short train ride to New Jersey. The plane stopped at eight cities to refuel from Newark to Sacramento where I was officially discharged. My buddy and I hitchhiked our way through Portland, Oregon, and Seattle, Washington, headed toward Whidbey Island. I stayed one night with relatives in Hillsborough, Oregon, before coming home as I had left . . . on a bus."

Bud was now home with family and friends on Whidbey Island. When he met his friend Jim Ronhaar at an OHHS football game, Bud knew he was really home when he hugged Jim. Like so many others, these men from Whidbey Island had put their lives on the line so that we can meet our friends at a hometown football game. He came home and married his high school sweetheart, Jo. God bless those who sacrifice their lives for that freedom and don't come home to their families, cheers, parades, or touchdowns.

Wesley "Wes" Rein Zylstra

From his **Oak Harbor High School Annual 1942**

In face of our present day troubles, we feel we should dedicate this page to a prayer for America. It is with the hope of an early peace that we of the Senior class of 1942 express our feeling in the words written by Pauline Streeter.

A PRAYER FOR AMERICA

War, war, that is the cry
And our present-day troubles are not just
  a lie
To offend peaceful nations is very unjust
But help us—Oh God—for defend we must.
When friendly feelings were being made
And peace-loving Americans were not afraid
Of invasion by others, when we didn't know
Help us—Oh God—to o'er power the foe.
For brave and fearless heroes, our boys
Many sad hearts inwardly filled with joys
Because of nobleness of which no one knew
Bless them God—they're men—through and
  through.
What's come has come, though unneedful it be
Enlarge mans' vision and help him to see
That all things worthwhile are gained through
  love,
Help us and bless us—Thou God, above.

Wes Zylstra, his cousin Bud Zylstra, and buddy Jim Ronhaar joined twenty-two other guys from Whidbey on the bus to Fort Lewis, Washington, in February 1943. Wes had just recently graduated early from Oak Harbor High School in December. At the age of seventeen, Wes worked part-time with Ray Tillish at the base as the Navy property clerk. His family doctor had told his parents that he had a defective heart, so he never played high school sports with his buddies and used the extra time for studying.

Ironically, Wes spent his teen years hunting, fishing, and dancing the jitterbug. Wes's family members were all musical and enjoyed singing together while traveling and dancing at the grange halls. He was allowed to go to any of the dances on the island and Skagit County, but not at Cornet Bay Precinct. They often went to the dances at San de Fuca every third Saturday of the month or the grange hall across the street from Smith Park. Pat Mullen was Wes's favorite partner.

Dorothy Meeter, his sweetheart, was a cheerleader at Oak Harbor High School. Wes joked about her wearing wooden shoes, which was his way of teasing Dotty about her dancing. They were not allowed to have a dance or dancing at their high school for any occasion. That was one of the restrictions when the land for the school was donated until 1948. Before Wes left for Fort Lewis, the pair entered a contest sponsored by Tommy Clark's band, the Tom Cats. It was a benefit to raise money to purchase air raid sirens for the city. Other contestants came as far away as Fort Casey, but it was Pat and Wes who jitterbugged their way into the hearts of the judges. They shared the two-silver-dollar prize. Wes still has his dollar.

"The Army doctors declared me fit for the infantry with or without a previously diagnosed heart problem. I rode on a train for the first time in my life to Camp Walters, Texas, for six weeks of basic training. There I stood freezing with the desert sand blowing in my face wearing my government issued uniform and size 12 Army boots. Because my feet were so long, I never had trouble getting a new pair.

"While I was stationed at Camp Walters, the recruits received their pay by standing in line alphabetically. Since Zylstra was always at the end, I and six other Z men were always the last to get paid. So we took off and played cards in the barracks until the pay line dwindled to the last dozen recruits. Then we casually got in line. Nobody noticed.

"On Sunday mornings, while others slept in, my buddy Ken Baker and I got up at 0600 and ran the obstacle course, came back, and showered. Then Ken went to the Protestant service at the base chapel and I went to the Catholic Mass in the gymnasium. Some afternoons we rented horses from a local rancher and played cowboy. It was in Fort Worth that I came across drinking fountains labeled black or white, my first experience with segregation. It was a startling reality. Other times we went to Mineral Wells, Texas. A place that was famous for their 'crazy water crystals.' We would have a nice dinner, talk with Army wives who worked there, and sipped chilled effervescent mineral water.

"After six months of basic training and another seven for infantry replacement training, I had orders to board another train and travel from Texas along the flooded Mississippi River Valley. Never before had I witnessed the devastation of this phenomenon. I watched families and their belongings on their rooftops from inside the train. The undisclosed destination of this troop train was Camp Shanago, Pennsylvania, in preparation for embarkation for overseas duty on another *Liberty* ship.

"Each soldier was issued either a white heavyweight hooded overcoat and white infantry boots and sent 'overseas' to Alaska. Or they were issued rain gear and ordered to get aboard another train headed to New Jersey. There hadn't been enough room on the ship for Europe. So we got passes from the corporal on duty at Camp Orange for a three-hour layover in New York City by passing him a buck. So we six young, naive, underage, uniformed tourists went to the downtown Taft Hotel to hear Vaughn Monroe and his band. There we met nice, but more experienced, underage city girls from Baltimore, Maryland. The girls decided the dancing, Cokes, and conversation had been fun, but they were hungry for an elegant dinner.

"While the girls left to dress for dinner, we got wise. Neither did we have the money for an expensive dinner with underage girls. We had to get back to Camp Orange. Ditching the girls while they were upstairs, we headed for the subway. After counting noses once on the subway, we were short a buddy. So we decided we had better go back and find him. Heading back to the subway, we saw our buddy still sound asleep on the backseat of the subway car. He had slept on the subway while it had made another complete loop.

"With my dog tags hung a Miraculous Medal of Mary given to me by a young lady while at Camp Shanago. My buddies and I were sent to the Port of Embarkation at Camp Patrick Henry, Virginia. There we boarded a *Liberty* boat and headed for North Africa. The boatload of replacement infantry troops landed in Casablanca, Morocco, and then boarded a French train "40 or 8 car" (40 GIs or 8 horses) traveling through to Bizerte, Tunisia. The Thirty-sixth Division of the Fifth Army Infantry replacement troops would be moved on to the Italian coast. While in Bizerte, I confiscated a Navy teaspoon and slipped it into my boot. The spoon would be my constant companion during my entire military service.

"Operation Avalanche, the assault landing for Salerno, was scheduled for the ninth of September. The Fifth Army Infantry, under Lt. Gen. Mark W. Clark, landed on a broad thirty-five-mile front that was easily defendable by the Germans. Six German divisions were positioned to cover all possible landing sites on the western coast from Rome south to the toe of Italy. While First Infantry troops approached the shore at Paestum, a loudspeaker from the landing area proclaimed in English, "Come on in and give up. We have

[The 36th Division insignia was adopted in 1918. The flint arrowhead represents the State of Oklahoma and the "T" is for Texas.

you covered." The Allied troops aggressively attacked the beach undaunted. This was their invitation to eleven months of hell.

"The German forces were well fortified in the mountains with heavy artillery, ample supplies, machine gun posts, dispersed tanks throughout the landing area, environmental camouflage, and the cold climate was a dependable ally of the German forces. In spite of the divisions' lack of combat experience and initial lack of organization, the beach area was successfully taken after nearly a month of intense combat.

"The enemy had a tactical advantage and was determined to force the Thirty-sixth Division back into the sea. The number of casualties was excessive that first week of hell. The American troops were spread too thin, until they received strong naval gunfire support, and the reinforcements and reorganized infantry units defeated all German attempts to retain control of the Salerno beachhead.

"The Thirty-sixth and the Forty-fifth divisions and the British Tenth Corps successfully drove a wedge into Hitler's Fortress. When the patrols of the Fifth and Eighth divisions linked up on September 16, 1943, the Germans began their retreat. Naples fell on October 1, and by the sixth, the Fifth Army troops were at the south bank of the Volturno River. We had to cover forty-eight miles in twenty-seven days. I didn't believe we could do it.

"The Third, Thirty-fourth, and Forty-fifth divisions were forced to cross the Volturno River during the twelfth and thirteenth nights of October. The weather was uncooperative: cold, rainy, and the swift water currents were deep enough to come up to their chests. We climbed each mountain in rain and mud usually under constant sniper fire and hidden mines. Progress was measured in yards between battle sites at Mignano, Venafro, Mt. Sammucro, San Pietro, Sen Vittore, Mt. Porchia, and Cervano. Casualty numbers increased daily on both sides.

"All casualties had to be carried back down these mountain mazes we had fought so hard to climb. Chaplains and medics constantly risked their lives trying to save the lives or the sanity of our men during combat. I usually had the somber duty of bringing back the casualties down those same mountains. All divisions were hemmed in on all three sides by the German forces. After months of combat and a couple of victories, we were able to break through the German lines. Every battle seemed to be bloodier and deadlier. We didn't have time to sleep or have nightmares. We just kept pushing and hoping that it would get easier. It never did.

"My division made the first bid by crossing the narrow Rapido River, south of town. This action was known as 'the Battle of Guts' and was the first time the Germans stopped our attacks and defended their strongest point in the 'Gustav Line.' I remember many of those they met in battle were SS men, Hitler's meanest and cruelest forces. When the brutality of combat lightened up, the Thirty-sixth Division had heavy losses and was forced back to where it had started. Field Marshal Sir Harold Alexander had complained frequently about the lack of landing craft and essential equipment. Alexander accepted the responsibility for leading the Allied forces in the prevailing conditions, which led to the pointless loss of lives within the British Fifty-sixth and American divisions. The tenacity of the German soldiers was remarkable."

During the next five long months, the Fifth Army wintered in the Apennines. Wes still bears the scars of those battles in Italy, not from bullets but from the many times his feet had been frozen. Taking Italy depended solely on the infantryman's ability to withstand the sticking, slimy mud that got in his shoes, hair, and chow. Cold rains, trench foot, and the casualties of S mines in the mud, Schu-mine 42, concrete mines, box mines, and Teller mines were constant enemies of the Thirty-sixth Division during the four months it took to capture Cassino. All supplies, ammunition, water, and rations had to be hauled up by mules. Then they carried the casualties back down the mountain. The wounded were transported to the evacuation units and/or hospitals.

"The dead were brought to a collection agency to be buried in a cemetery. The worst task that I had to do was carry the body of the man who had been my buddy since boot camp at Camp Walters, Texas. He had been killed instantly when a German shell made a direct hit. The impact of the explosion made wallpaper of his body against the stony walls of his foxhole during the battle on Mt. Lungo. It's a battle that sticks in my memory too. You can only imagine cleaning the remnants of a friend's indistinguishable body parts off of the rocks and carrying them over the logs, in the mud, and ducking sniper's bullets all the way to the collection agency.

"The 'Krauts' stopped the attacks with an invigorated determination to push the Fifth Army back into the sea. For the men who patrolled the lines in the rain and freezing cold, it was essential for their survival to walk with caution along rocky pathways, sweep out mines, or ambushes. I can't forget the sounds of the rapid fire machine guns fired at will by Germans, who were well protected in their caves, compared to the single shots from infantry rifles which conserved ammunition. The sound of the last gun fired indicated the victor. The ability to employ a bayonet well and throw hand grenades accurately was mandatory for survival as well. Acute senses, adrenaline, my ability to use my gun, bayonet, and the Lord was all I had to defend myself.

"Most of the time I dug a small cave on the floor in the back of my foxholes to keep my feet dryer, but we constantly had wet and muddy socks, which invited trench foot. The combat action in Italy was worse than in France or Germany. There are a lot of good soldiers buried in Italy. We carried a detailed map exactly where they had been buried. There was never even a moment in which any soldier could relax or take the time to pray. We had to pay attention all the time. The infantryman's body and mind on the front line was in a state of continuous high adrenaline, constant apprehension, and fear that the next bullet would mean certain death under these horrific conditions.

"The soldier on the front line had to be wary of every unaccountable sound. There was no defense from a sniper or an enemy on the flank of your foxhole. A split-second decision to attempt to save a wounded buddy meant life or death for one or both. During a lull in the battle, the wounded calling for help had German accents, a trick by the enemy hoping to lure another victim within killing range.

"Our division continued to hammer away at the defenders of the Gustav Line. On January 30, 1944, Thirty-fourth Division repulsed a powerful counterattack by German forces. By February 13, the

New Zealand Corps took over the positions of the Thirty-Fourth Division. By March 28, the Thirty-fourth Division replaced the Third Division in the fight to break through the German lines at the Anzio beachhead.

"On May 18, the Polish forces, that seemed to be more adaptive to these mountainous conditions, captured and leveled the 1,500-year-old monastery of Monte Cassino that was built in AD 529 by the monks of St. Benedict. This was a turning point in the invasion. I remember the only occasion I heard a radio broadcast was near Anzio. The division had been on the move and we sat down to rest in the dark. The password for that night 'airline stewardess' had been whispered from one man to the next. As we listened to the Axis Sally during her propaganda-loaded broadcast say, 'Why don't you, brave men go home to your wives and sweethearts. While you're over here, they are sleeping with cowardly 4-Fs. By the way, the password for tonight is airline stewardess.' At the time it was demoralizing to hear this propaganda and even more so to hear her give them the so-called secret password.

"Under Commander Walker, I was a part of one of two regiments that infiltrated enemy lines via isolated areas of the Germans. We broke through the German ring that had been closing in on the Allied forces at the Anzio beachhead. The two regiments formed right and left flank forces behind the Germans. On June 1, I was with the right flank of the regiment that launched an offensive towards the north in the direction of Valmontone. The left-flanking regiment of the Eighty-fifth Division attacked Monte Ceraso, meeting strong resistance. With the Gustav Line breached, the Germans withdrew to the Gothic Line and gradually disengaged the aggressive attacks. June 3, Allied forces advanced along the whole front in Italy."

The Krauts were badly defeated, giving the Fifth Army an opportunity to move rapidly toward Rome. By June 4, 1944, the special task forces had taken the city. On June 5, triumphant Allied forces were given a euphoric welcome in Rome.

"Only a third of my company had been allowed to go back into Rome, and I wasn't included in that group. Captain John Goetcher didn't give permission for any of the other men to go. What he said implied that if anyone got caught sneaking back into Rome, he would have to 'throw the book at them, so don't get caught.' As a devout Catholic, I yearned to see the Vatican."

"Anzio Annie" had been one of the Germans' greatest assets, the two railroad guns that were rolled out on tracks, which together became known as one. They were positioned safely in the Alban hills. Twenty-four soldiers could stand shoulder to shoulder on the barrel. The K5 (E) was one of the finest artillery pieces made. It weighed 218 tons and the gun could fire a 255-kilogram shell to a range of 62 kilometers.

Wes retells a story by Al Johnson, Master Chief, who was aboard the admiral's gig carrying as an observer, Prime Minister Winston Churchill. The boat had been anchored in the harbor off the coast of Anzio when "Anzio Annie" took aim at the Navy artillery fleet. The shells landed close enough to the admiral's gig to create waves strong enough to move the boat within the harbor. "Anzio Annie" now resides in Maryland as a prize of war.

"Gen. Alexander McCarrell Patch became the commanding general of the new Seventh Army. After the infantry forces' success in Cassino and Anzio, many of the troops were pulled out of Italy to participate in the invasion of Southern France. I was among those chosen to volunteer. On August 15, 1944, the Seventh Army personnel made the crossing in transport ships (LCIs), and Operation Dragoon meant for me to hit the beach at Frejus of Southern France.

"The Seventh Army traveled up the Rhone Valley on foot, armed with 'Long Toms' 150-millimeter artillery guns, well aware of the mines that had been left. Ninety-four thousand men landed during the course of a day, quickly establishing complete control. The men had to rely on the Army Corps of Engineers to mark the minefields with white tape for their safety. Unfortunately, the white tape was often moved. The Seventh Army was occasionally escorted by U.S. tanks and got air support to destroy the mined tunnels and bridges. Before the end of August, our forces and the French Resistance controlled the mouth of the Rhone River to Nice. Forty-eight thousand German soldiers and four thousand enemy vehicles were captured.

"The Fifth Armored Army and the Seventh Army escaped capture the corridor units of the Germans and continued to work their way through the French Alps toward Germany's Siegfried Line. By August 22, the Thirty-sixth Division has taken Grenoble without meeting any resistance. On August 24 in Paris, the German General Dietrich von Choltitz rejected Hitler's orders to burn all of Paris down to the ground (the public squares, museums, and bridges of Paris). Rather than face the fuehrer or the British, French Resistance, and America's Army troops, General Dietrich von Choltitz surrendered to French General Leclerc.

"I got more than my share of kisses and hugs from the French girls. A buddy had given me a little strategy should I be a part of a force liberating a German-held town, 'Always position yourself on the outside of a division when marching into a French city.'

"I managed to work my way to the edge of the throng of infantry entering Paris. Sure enough I got more than my share of hugs and kisses. There was a particularly attractive French girl accompanied by a young Frenchman. Well, I got that first passionate kiss, and it was worth weaving around the division to make a second pass at the same girl. On the third time around, her fellow was wise to my nonmilitary maneuver and made it clear there would be no third passionate hug and kiss. I went to the Follies Bergere starring Maurice Chevalier. I had never seen such splendor as this theater. Oh, the girls were beautiful and nice, but what both amazed and thrilled me the most was watching the center circle of the ceiling being lowered. Suspended from the ceiling was a golden birdcage and inside was a scantily clad singer with a feather boa that might have covered her. She sang, "I'm Only a Bird in a Gilded Cage."

[Presented to Wes for Distinguished Military Valor and the Liberation of Paris]

"During my only three days in Paris, I met an English girl who had been a prisoner of the Germans. She gave me coffee, donuts, and her personal stationery on which I could write home. She gave me a ruby ring that I still wear and remember her fondly. I was also invited to a private club where I was given a royal reception. I had been a real dancer, and this wonderful music made me forget the cold and wet weather, and the mud that had been deep enough to come up to my knees in Italy. For a few wonderful hours I forgot the pain of my 'trench foot' and the Germans who had literally used our divisions for target practice. But I knew the war with Germany was not over, no matter how much I prayed for an end.

"While heading back to the front line, I caught sight of my cousin Bud Zylstra riding through Luneville, France, the Army Command Headquarters with one of his officers. We had little opportunity to talk, but I felt for the first time reassured that we would survive this hell. I would live to see my cousin and home again. Bud had promised to come back that way again when he had more time and a pass to wherever my unit was assigned.

"The Allies swiftly headed north up the Rhone Valley capturing Lyon on September 3. We were met with fire and hand-to-hand combat. The men helped themselves to a token reward whenever they could snitch a green pepper to cut up and mix in with their mess kit meals. Then the armies set out to strike the Siegfried Line. Western France was returned to the French patriots. We liberated Bordeaux, the Third and Seventh units were driving closer and closer to an assault on Germany. We crossed the German border on September 11, 1944."

Under the command of General Patch, the Seventh Army reached the Rhine River before Thanksgiving Day, November 23, 1944, with an intact bridge, crossing the German's Siegfried Line (the West Wall) to complete history's first recorded winter crossing of the Vosges Mountains (for which the unit received a Presidential Citation).

On November 27, General Patch had orders to take the U.S. Seventh Army and turn north once again to support Patton's Third Army in the capture of the Saar Basin. The Germans increased their blows and continued to win minor successes. The division continued active patrols and held the line against fierce German counterattacks. The Germans' retreat was bitter and vindictive; they had cut down the timber along the upper mountain ridges. The division had to climb over terrain covered with logs that resembled giant 'pickup sticks.' The units re-orientated themselves from offensive to defensive.

However, the SS had relatively little military experience and advanced in suicidal open waves, cursing and screaming at the U.S. Infantry. German "screaming meemies" were again used during this campaign. They were about eight inches in diameter and about fifteen inches long and appeared to be electronically ignited from multi-mounted racks. A dozen exhaust holes at an angle to their bases provided forward propulsion and rotation, generated by an expanding liquid gas. Their slow rate of speed permitted a loud whistling to reach the ear well before the rocket did.

When spring finally arrived, three Allied armies crossed the Rhine River and General Patch's Seventh Army led the attack on the Siegfried Line. While the Seventh Army controlled parts of the Black Forest, Bavaria was captured, including Hitler's Alpine residence, the Berghof, the Eagle's Nest near the village of Berchtesgaden. Wes would be in Salzburg, Austria, when his commander General Fred Walker received word on May 8, 1945, the war in Europe was over.

[GERMAN SURRENDER: The end of the war and unit of the U.S. Fifth Army make contact with the U.S. Seventh Army pushing south through the Brenner Pass. Caught in the middle, the German Army tries to find its way home after the surrender on 2 May, 1945. The Military History of World War II.]

"In Salzburg, a buddy and I made unauthorized friends and visitations with a gracious German family. We brought Army coffee, the family furnished stationery for the guys to write home, and then they'd roll back the rug and waltzed to the music of Strauss on an old hand-cranked record player. Their daughter Hannah Laura was delightful and promised not to cut her hair until I returned. My parents sent them care packages from Whidbey Island. But my parents were looking forward to having their son home again. Hannah Laura could keep her hair.

"I was looking forward to the only three days of R & R since my escapade in New York City at the Taft Hotel. I brought home souvenirs from my service in the Army, a .38-caliber Belgium pistol, an SS Captain's dagger with the inscription 'My heart is true,' the Miraculous Medal of Mary on my dog tags, nightmares, memories of seeing the Vatican, Notre Dame, the Eiffel Tower, the scars on my feet, and a Navy issued spoon from Tunisia."

General Eisenhower sent those, like Wes, who had served him well, into two or more theater operations in Italy, France, and/or Germany home rather than to the Pacific. S.Sgt. Wes Zylstra was discharged from the Army at Fort Lewis, Washington on December 15, 1945. He returned home to his family, buddy Jim Ronhaar, and cousin Bud Zylstra on Whidbey Island. When I asked Wes if he ever would want to go back to France or Italy, he was very quick to answer, "When the Statue of Liberty has turned around."

I took that to mean *no*. Any regrets?

"I regret not going to a university for a degree when I got out of the Army. I don't regret leaving Betty Davis, the girl I met in Youngstown, Pennsylvania, before I left for Italy. Betty had sent a letter every day and enclosed a stick of gum. She's the wonderful girl who gave me the Miraculous Medal of Mary that I still wear."

Wes was now a veteran of three European theater military invasions; he spent three years of youth honorably in the U.S. Infantry. Furthermore, Dorothy, his high school sweetheart, was waiting for him to come home so they could be married. Without a doubt, Dotty was the love of his life; they were married sixty-two years. Wes followed her within five months of her death. Your many friends miss you.

In Loving Memory...

Wesley Rein Zylstra

September 25, 1922
~
January 28, 2009

In Loving Memory...

Dorothy M. "Dottie" Zylstra

April 21, 1926
~
October 5, 2008

My Journey with Uncle Sam
Authored by
Sgt. John J. "Jim" Ronhaar

I chose to include most of Jim's account of life on Whidbey Island, military training and discipline programs (boot camp), as well as his combat memoirs of World War II as he wrote them. This interview includes direct excerpts from his book *My Journey with Uncle Sam* (his complete published legacy).

On the Home Front

The West Coast line of America was caught up in a frenzy of preparation to defend our homeland from invasion. Japan had already bombed the Alaskan islands of Adak and Attu. Both Canadian and American coastlines bordering the Pacific Ocean, including Whidbey Island, were alerted to the possibility of an invasion by the Japanese. Blackout curtains were required for every home. No lights were allowed to be visible after dark for fear of being seen by enemy planes flying overhead. Night driving on many roads was to be traveled under blackout conditions, using only parking lights. If the parking lights were deemed to be too bright and visible, fifty-candlepower bulbs were installed into the circuit under the hood to dim the lights. A state patrol car was stationed on Canoe Island at the Deception Pass Bridge twenty-four hours a day. Gun emplacements were manned twenty-four hours a day by troops from Fort Casey in strategic places along the west side of the island, the Reservation Bay area, and on Canoe Island.

Men and women were recruited to stand watch in shifts to identify and record every airplane they could see or hear. Also recorded was the direction in which they were headed. Others were armed with shotguns and/or rifles in order to patrol all west-side beaches of the island for submarines and/or other enemy amphibious landings. Since our family didn't possess such weapons, I opted for air patrol at a lookout station located near John Overway's farm in Clover Valley prior to the expanding Whidbey Island Naval Air Station at Ault Field. I worked at the Oak Harbor Transfer Company (forerunner to Oak Harbor Freight Lines) in Oak Harbor, dated my high school sweetheart, Ardie Vogt, earlier in the evenings. I managed to stay awake because I never knew when I would get caught napping by friend or foe.

In 1942, the Navy began buying farmland by the thousands of acres near Crescent Harbor, Clover Valley, Swantown, and Oak Harbor. Many displaced farm families were relocated in Skagit and Whatcom Counties. Appeals for dissatisfied landowners were for naught. Longtime families were uprooted and traumatized when they were forced to leave their friends, families, churches, and schoolmates to start over.

On at least one occasion, a born pilot, Bernie Hingston was reported for flying under the Deception Pass Bridge. In 1939, Bernie had joined the Royal Canadian Air Force in support of England. But his assignment was to watch for any Japanese assault forces along the coast of Washington and Canadian shores. He was a great guy.

I had graduated from Oak Harbor High School in June of 1941 at the age of eighteen. Employed by the Oak Harbor Transfer part-time since age fifteen by Gus Vander Pol, I was trusted to drive his new 1942 Ford truck with a two-speed axle. A bed for hauling lumber was installed. The truck was plain in appearance, without reflective chrome, and painted dark green, except for the cream-colored grill. I hauled the very first load of lumber onto the new Naval Air Station when construction began and thousands of board feet of lumber thereafter. The Austin Construction Company built the very first office building on the base. Sometime after the war, Chuck Bos purchased and moved this building to his property located on Barrington Avenue and converted it into a four-unit apartment building.

The letter from Uncle Sam's Draft Board arrived October 13, 1942, one day after my twentieth birthday. Since Oak Harbor Transfer was heavily involved in the hauling of essential materials for the war effort and equipment for the new base, my bosses requested that I apply for a deferment. It was a difficult decision; I was in love with Ardie, and a deferment would allow me another ninety days at home. Knowing that the war was increasing daily, other young men were being wounded or killed, and that I was safe at home gnawed at my conscience.

During my deferment, I drove to Seattle on a regular basis, hauling dressed turkeys to Seattle markets such as Acme Poultry, owned by Morris Pollack. Our return trips brought a variety of materials to Oak Harbor, most of it to the Austin Company on the new base. The need increased for more men, equipment, and trucks for Oak Harbor Transfer, which was now restricted to purchasing only used trucks, two semitrailers, and two four-wheeled trailers. Ironically, while riding the bus to Seattle for my physical, I noticed an Oak Harbor Transfer truck parked beside the road north of Seattle. As it turned out, the driver had simply stolen the truck and drove it until it ran out of gas.

Jack Hamming and John Terpstra were not granted a deferment. I joined them along with Joe Tyhuis, Bernard Riksen, Bud Zylstra, Wes Zylstra, Harold Reinstra, Con Vander Woude, Mel Simmons, Troy McKinney, Hobart Rorrer, Don Wade, and others from Whidbey Island. After a long sleepless night, I bid my sweetheart and family good-bye on February 19, 1943. The weather epitomized the feeling roiling in our stomachs. Our minds held dark, cold, and foggy thoughts about those we might never see again, and an excitement that would not be denied.

We were not accustomed to the treatment we received at Fort Lewis. We were herded like cattle, learned to obey orders without question, and inoculated, with square needles, for every dreaded disease known to man. We were issued clothes and shoes with steel plates on the heels. I guess they expected my size 10½ feet to grow into those 12's. Two pairs of socks finally got the fit as good as it would get. Every morning we were rousted out of our bunks in the dark, told to "police the area and pick up anything that doesn't grow." I learned quickly to use my eyes in the dark after picking up an oyster that someone else had thrown up.

The Army ran us through a series of aptitude tests to determine if we could put round pegs in a square hole. They determined that I was qualified to receive training in Message Center Operations. Along with many other men, including Joe Tyhuis, Jack Hamming, Hobart Roher, and I were sent to Camp Roberts, California, an Infantry Replacement Training Center. Bernard Riksen and Bud Zylstra were assigned to the Army Air Corps (Air Force); John Terpstra was sent to Fort Douglas, Utah, for medical duties. During my training, I was told repeatedly how lucky I was to be there instead of being shipped to an Infantry Rifle Company.

I remember going through Klamath Falls, Oregon, on my first train ride. Arriving in Oakland, California, we were taken to San Francisco by the ferry *Sacramento* before the completion of the Oakland Bay Bridge. Those ferries were later purchased by the state of Washington to navigate the Puget Sound waters. On a rainy February day, we arrived at Camp Roberts, near San Miguel and Paso Robles. Assigned to Company C of the Eighty-seventh Training Battalion, I learned to send and receive Morse code, operate radios, code and decode messages, and read aerial maps. We spent hours learning to march in close order drill, the manual of arms, marching to cadence, hand-to-hand combat using bayonets, pole climbing, and lots of hiking. I recall one of the worst cross-country hikes took us through rain-soaked clay that clung to our boots, making them heavier and heavier. My size 12 boots just about wore me out.

Whining, pranks, short sheeting, itching powder, homesickness, and GI bathing was the disorder of the day. When everyone had had enough of one particular recruit's aversion to personal hygiene and bathing, he was stripped naked. They dragged him kicking and screaming to the showers where they applied GI soap and scrub brushes until his skin was a rosy pink. Since I was the tallest man in my squad, I led every marching drill or hike. Not much thought was given to the short-legged guys at the rear of the line. They had to walk faster and harder just to stay in formation, and there was always a corporal at the rear to prod them along if they lagged behind.

I grew up during the Great Depression and watched my parents work long days. Often they worked at several jobs to provide food for our family of eight. Mom used everything; nothing went to waste. The few scraps went to our dog. However, when I was assigned KP, it was a terrible shock for me to see the huge amount of food that was thrown away after every meal. Tubs of beautiful, delicious mashed potatoes with butter and other leftovers, my mother would have had a fit. Local hog farmers bid for the privilege of collecting it for their hogs.

When we first arrived, we were issued 1903 bolt-action rifles from World War I. When we were issued brand-new Garand M1 rifles completely saturated with a heavy protective coating of cosmoline. The best way to remove the coating was to immerse the rifle in boiling water. But the water was just warm. It took us the better part of a day to get them cleaned and ready for inspection. Even then, a number of men were "gigged" and had to do the job over.

The military brass has a way to fill you with fear and trembling when it comes to obeying rules and respecting authority. We were told, "Never let this weapon out of your sight or your possession. It can be a matter of life or death." One day I was given a key and an armload of maps to deliver to a classroom. All I had to do was to run into the classroom, dump the maps on the table. I opted to leave my rifle for that brief moment, WRONG! When I returned for my rifle, the commanding general was standing with my rifle. I just got a lecture, but I wasn't disciplined then. Stories about white-glove inspections were just as imposing as they portrayed. Discipline was always a valuable lesson of fear and discipline. Possibly spending a hot afternoon digging a 4'× 4'× 4' hole in the middle of the company area.

One of the more exciting bits of training occurred while crawling under barbed wire with live machine gun fire overhead, located in a sandy riverbed. After a lengthy lecture with many warnings, and actual demonstrations, then we're cautioned to keep the sand out of our rifles. A rifle filled with sand is of no use. Later in combat, this lesson helped me numerous times, as I later encountered many situations when it took a lot of self-discipline to remain reasonably calm. Another bit of training was going through the gas chamber. The tear gas, for those who panicked, brought on coughing and crying. It was another memorable experience.

As a private, I received $50.00 per month, out of which $6.50 was taken for my GI insurance paying $10,000.00 to my parents in the event I was killed, plus laundry charges, and whatever I spent at the PX. I also bought a savings bond each month.

June 17, 1943, upon completion of thirteen weeks of basic training, my departure from Camp Roberts arrived, but none of us had any idea of where we were being sent. After a train ride from Southern California, we arrived at Camp Polk, Louisiana. At one of the sidings in Arizona, we heard from some of the men in the Tank Corps engaged in desert training under General George Patton. The desert heat must have been unbearable as they reported over 1,500 men being AWOL. It was hot enough sitting there long enough to let a train pass, let alone being out in the sand and sagebrush all day, every day, and in an enclosed tank.

From Camp Polk, I was assigned to the Eighty-eighth Infantry Division, one of three divisions sent to Louisiana for the next two months for simulated combat training, called Army Maneuvers. I was immediately assigned to Company A of the 313th Engineer Battalion as an assistant radioman under Pvt. Henry Maynard. The irony was that he knew nothing about radios, and we had only a receiver that didn't work. In this outfit everything and everyone was sloppy. They gave the appearance of a bunch of convicts.

Nothing I had learned in basic training had prepared me as an engineer. I soon learned that the main purpose of the combat engineers was to keep the roads open, building and repairing bridges for the transporting food and ammunition to the boys at the front line. I became proficient in demolition work, clearing land mines from the roads and fields, knot tying and rope splicing. Army maneuvers were no picnic; it meant rising before daylight for breakfast, a peanut butter and grape jelly sandwich for lunch. It was a long time between meals, but this was fine eating compared to what we had ahead of us in real combat.

Upon completion of maneuvers, the 88th had earned the privilege of being stationed at Fort Sam Houston, Texas a premier duty station. All equipment was cleaned and readied for the long trip by truck convoy to San Antonio and Fort Sam. While there, many of the men were able to secure furloughs to the homes of their parents, sweethearts, or wives. But before I could buy a ticket, all furloughs were canceled and all men were recalled to duty. We knew that we soon would be going overseas because of the last minute of accelerated training at the firing range and preparing all our equipment for transporting. Instead of a ticket home, I bought an engagement ring and mailed it to Ardie. I knew very little about diamonds. The first was so small; I bought her another when I got home.

Convicts?
No gravel. Cpt. Lee Wisdom
Breaking rocks with sledge hammer

Building our winter home
Courtland Wright
Lee Wisdom
Jim Ronhaar

**Sgt. Jim Ronhaar
Winter home 1944**

**Platoon Sgt.
Sidney Bodie**

Pvt. Armando Cota

One of the bright spots in my stay at Fort Sam occurred when I received word that 2nd Lt. Lawrence Dykers had been assigned to G Company, 350th Infantry Regiment of the Eighty-eighth Division. In the short time that we were at Fort Sam, Doc and I got to see each other three or four times. It was a sad day when we boarded the train in early November as we were going overseas. We saw some marvelous country and a lot of beautiful plantations.

The port of embarkation at Hampton Roads was made up of a bunch of shanties covered with tar paper. It was cold, dark, dreary, raining, and foggy; nor was there much for us to do. We received a number of lectures, warnings, and threats regarding the importance of secrecy surrounding crossing the German submarine-patrolled Atlantic Ocean. I bought a box of Hershey milk chocolate bars with almonds, which I nibbled at during the nineteen-day trip to Casablanca.

The military's decision to feed us dehydrated food such as potatoes, beets, carrots, and powdered eggs and milk only made the close confinement and crowded conditions add to the miseries of those who were already seasick. That was our inauguration for two more years of dehydrated food and lots of powdered ice cream mix while we were at the front lines with no refrigeration.

While boarding a Liberty ship, the *Albert Carrig,* in Virginia, we were marched aboard in alphabetical order and herded to the cargo holds surrounded by bunks, six high from floor to ceiling. Our bunks were assigned according to our place in line. I was assigned a bunk so dark and dank that it resembled a hole in a coal mine. But I spotted an empty bunk on the top which had enough room to sit up and read or play cards, and a light overhead, and no one could step on me.

We were told that there were over a hundred ships in our convoy across the Atlantic dodging German U-boats. I wonder how many extra days it required for us to zigzag our way while escorted by armed naval ships and a destroyer or two. After one week, toilet drains plugged and overflowed for three or four days and boots were needed just to maneuver. The smell of it was bad enough to send some of us up on the bow of the boat and huddle together and watch the wall of water cascade over us. The trick was to get to and from the deck or the bow between waves and stay dry.

Once we reached North Africa, we were surrounded on every side by thousands of Arabs in their native garments, and we had no idea how they felt about American soldiers. I bought several mementos to send home to Ardie, some of which we still have. We landed at Casablanca, Morocco, December 1, 1944. The cold in Africa surprised me, but we didn't waste any time getting back in shape. After being assigned our tents, our next job was to take our mattress bags and fill them with straw that had been provided for this purpose. The more straw, the more insulation we had between our kidneys and the cold ground. It was during this time that Lt. Lawrence Dykers and I were able to spend a Sunday or two together talking shop, exchanging information from home, and reminiscing about Oak Harbor.

During this time, I was sent to attend a Bailey Bridge School to learn how to construct a bridge of this type. Since the school was in session every day, the work area was a quagmire of ankle to mid-calf deep in mud. The ingenious Bailey bridge was invented by an Englishman that went together like Tinker Toys or an Erector Set. During combat, many of the old stone bridges were destroyed by artillery and bombing. Whenever a bypass could not be built, a Bailey bridge was assembled to keep the flow of supplies, ammunition, and rations flowing to the front line.

The complete bridge is built on rollers with the nose portion built at an angle resembling a sled runner. It was rolled into place as parts were added. Using heavy jacks, it was raised to remove the rollers. Then replacement footings were more solid and permanent. The construction area required enough open space to allow for a counterbalance. The one we built was done at night while under enemy fire. Short of space because of a curve in the road, to get the needed counterbalance, we drove our big D-8 bulldozer onto the bridge, backing it as far as possible to keep the nose heavy bridge from going into the river. With the added weight of the dozer, we had to push that much harder to move the bridge forward.

Once the bridge was finished, we were given breakfast and allowed to sleep most of the day as we had been working for thirty-six hours. But under stress, someone forgot to pin two bottom panels together. This meant we had to add another row of panels on top of those already there. The panels weighed six hundred pounds each and required six men using special carrying bars to move them from place to place. Because of the error, we had to lift them to the second layer.

Approximately January 1, 1944, Brigadier General Paul W. Kendall and every regimental, battalion, company, and platoon commander, plus every platoon sergeant, were being sent to Italy. It was time for the Eighty-eighth Division to move to Italy where we would join the Thirty-sixth, Forty-fifth, and First armored divisions already in heavy combat. There they were assigned temporary billets, commensurate of their rank, with units already in combat during the infamous Rapido River crossing where the extremely high casualty rate suffered by the Thirty-sixth Infantry Division came very near to ending General Mark Clark's military career. My good friend Wes Zylstra and members of the Thirty-sixth Infantry Division were also there at the icy Rapido River. The boys of the Thirty-sixth Infantry stumbled through night-screened minefields with assault boats on their shoulders down to the river. They crawled across a thickly iced, rail-less bridge over a bloody little stream and fell under a hail of gun, mortar, and automatic fire in the gallant attempt to establish a bridgehead.

I had to be treated at the Division Hospital; they were afraid I had meningitis, but like over fifty others, I was suffering from severe dysentery caused by spoiled hamburger. I

Climax of a campaign, Fifth Army troops pass through an ancient arch to enter Rome from the south.

even received a great welcome from the company commander when I returned to the company area. Arriving at the staging area in Oran, Algeria, I was assigned guard duty from the advantageous point of the latrine. The next morning we were loaded on trucks for the trip to pier and port of embarkation. I was given a square wooden box in which I could relieve myself. With nothing but liquids left in my body, I was embarrassed to find myself trying to balance my bare butt on an empty ration box. Then watch my body wastes flow from the cracks in the box, along the bed of the truck, in full view of my friends, and out over the tailgate. All this because they wouldn't allow me to use the latrine! An hour or two later after being herded aboard a British ship, I was finally able to shower, change clothes, and see the ship's doctor. What a lousy way to go to war.

The Real Thing

The four-day trip across the Mediterranean and Tyrrhenian seas was uneventful, except for the possibility of German submarines, which kept us a little tense. It was a real eye opener to see the devastation heaped upon Naples harbor by the Allied bombers. The harbor was littered with the hulks of sunken ships of every size, which, in a sense, now served as piers to which our ship tied up. To reach shore, we traveled over wooden walkways built over the top of sunken ships.

After spending a night in a bombed-out building, we were trucked to the small town of Santa Maria Aversa a few miles north of Naples. We were once again housed in six-man tents located near a farmer's olive grove. Blessed with a "liberated" stove and a fry pan in our tent, it offered opportunities for "liberated fresh eggs and chickens" from a neighboring farmer. When he confronted our company commander, Captain Gerald Snow, demanding recompense, Captain Snow replied, "My men don't steal." The stove proved to be a godsend when the men needed hot packs for drawing out blood poisoning, minor infections, and conjunctivitis.

My buddy Jerry Rogers was a gifted self-taught musician. He told of how he and his mother played music together. Before we left Fort Sam and San Antonio, our platoon supplied the money for Jerry to buy a guitar. There had been many sessions of listening to his playing or enjoying group singing on the ship, in Africa, and now in Italy. Once reaching Italy where accordions were plentiful, it didn't take long before Jerry had one of his own. It was amazing how quickly he became proficient. Jerry had to carry the guitar and the accordion in addition to everything else. One of the benefits of being in the Engineers Division is we rode and stowed things on the trucks rather than walked like the infantry. Most of us had found waterproof ammo boxes or containers in which to keep our letters, stationery, and private mementos.

Each engineer squad of twelve men had a four-wheel drive, tandem axle, two-ton rig, with a canvas top over the cab, a front-mounted winch, and a hydraulic lift for the bed. Each truck carried four chests, which doubled as benches when traveling. One chest, the Pioneer Chest, contained picks, shovels, bars, wrecking bars, posthole diggers, axes, brush hooks, a chain saw, and miscellaneous other tools. The Carpenter Chest contained hammers, saws, hatches, levels, squares, and other carpenter tools. The shorter nail chest contained an ample supply of different sizes of nails and spikes, and the Demolition Chest was filled with TNT blocks, nitromone, primer cord, blasting caps, fuses, wire cutters, and crimper for crimping caps to fuse cords or primer cord and mine detectors. When necessary, everything was unloaded and the truck was used to haul gravel. Because of the length of the truck bed, a folding section near the front was raised to keep the weight of the load over the axles. It was a great and versatile truck.

The night of March 5, 1944, was a very frightening night when we first went into the combat zone. We were driven to our positions just across the Garigliano River near the town of Castleforte, located in the Liri valley along the Casino-Minturno front. This is what we had been trained for and had been hearing about since basic training. I guess it would have been pretty frightening if we could have seen where we were going during daylight hours.

It was bad enough under the cover of darkness. As we drove, no one was talking. All of us were very frightened as we could hear our artillery guns sending death and destruction upon the enemy. At that point we were unable to distinguish between "outgoing" and "incoming" mail, as shelling came to be known. With all the rain, everything was very muddy. There was no way you could sneak up on anyone as each step gave a loud sucking noise as we walked. We were housed in deserted buildings with no furnishings, sleeping on the floors.

I do not know how these things come together, but the very first night at the front, I was assigned to a walking post on guard duty.

Not knowing which direction the enemy was supposed to be or how close he was, it was pretty scary. As my company commander, Captain Snow, was walking around checking to see that everyone was settling in, I dutifully challenged him as he approached me. Knowing him to be a fair man, I suggested my post become a standing post, as walking was so noisy. He concurred, thanked me for the suggestion, and slogged off through the mud. He was also kind enough to point out the direction of where the Germans were supposed to be.

Captured German troops were dazed at the savagery of the 88th's first attack.

Later that night, my heart went to my mouth as I heard this strange sound coming closer. I prepared myself to shoot. It turned out to be a mule train loaded with water cans, food, and ammunition, and headed for the front line infantry troops who needed it. I wouldn't want to have been involved with a mule train. An American officer was in charge, but most of the men used were loyal Italian patriots supporting the Allies any way they could. Many men and mules paid with their lives as the Germans, realizing they carried critical materials to strengthen their enemies, regularly shelled the mule trains.

With the arrival of the daylight, we were able to look over the countryside and get a better understanding of our location. We were shocked to learn we were under German observation as they held the high hills to the north, particularly Mt. Damiano, a bald stone mountain as the highest point. As the days went by, we learned to relax a little, found we could throw a football, work on the road, and a few other things, without drawing enemy fire. It was a very weird feeling to know the enemy was observing everything we did.

The roads in rural Italy were made to accommodate ox carts and light vehicles, so our heavy trucks soon tore them apart, making them into a quagmire and filling the ditches with mud too thick to run. One day, our platoon was ordered out to clean the ditches for better run off from the road. Our only tool for this job was a number 2 shovel. Buckets would have been better. Even gravity seemed to be our enemy while everything shoveled out flowed right back. We became irritated at the senselessness of the project. That night we were given the job of digging a ditch across the road and inserting a wooden culvert to better improve drainage.

When it came time to place a heavy culvert into the ditch, Cpl. Frank Waite failed to give explicit instructions as to his expectations and also failed to call the cadence for us to work together as a unit in the dark. This resulted in disgust and anger as all of us were pushing and pulling independently, rather than together as a team. Being short fused; I took over, giving instructions and counting the cadence, causing the culvert to be easily put in place. When it was backfilled, we were through for the night and returned to our rooms.

Expecting to be reprimanded for my angry and assertive action, I was shocked when I received a promotion. I argued that I was not the right man for the job. My superiors refuted every argument I put forth. Finally, we agreed on a temporary assignment. That assignment lasted nine months until I was promoted to sergeant. Sergeant Bodie and I developed a great friendship and a good working relationship. I didn't have to worry about being overworked as he was like an old grandma having to oversee everything himself.

When the Eighty-eighth Division went into combat, we relieved a unit of the British Army whose men were from India. One of these Indian soldiers, carrying a barber's kit, came into our company area asking in very broken English, "Haircut, Johnny?" I was the first one in line having my hair cut as short as the clippers could get.

As the barber was cutting Maki's hair and seeing a scaly head that hadn't been washed in a very long time, he asked, "How many year no wash, Johnny?" Later, when none of us had opportunity to wash for a while, someone was bound to ask, "How many year no wash, Johnny?" That usually brought a chuckle from the others.

One of the duties of the combat engineers is road maintenance, caring for roads from the front lines back to where corps engineers take over. When we needed gravel, regardless of being continually under the watchful eyes of the Germans, we worked in the dark. We knocked down and loaded stone buildings into our trucks and spread them out on the roads. These buildings were in "no man's land", so we worked hard and fast to sledgehammer the building until it collapsed. Then we quickly loaded up, called in the security, and hightailed it out of there. Since there was no way this could be done quietly, our hearts were in our mouths all the time we worked.

I don't know who blew the old stone bridges, the Allies or the Germans, but the Germans knew when they were blown. So they would shell it quite regularly while we worked to rebuild them. Their barrages caused many delays, angering the infantry officers whose men were really getting bombarded and suffering high casualties. The regimental infantry officers were unkind and threatening in their remarks as their men were suffering a high number of casualties. Their non-compromising attitude resulted in a lecture by the division commander, General John Sloan. It was pretty hard to do a good job when you're so tired you can hardly stand, let alone the stress of trying to stay among the living, then being cursed because the job isn't being done fast enough. Knowing that men on the front line are dying because your squad can't get the job done while being fired upon by the enemy.

It was under these combat conditions that we suffered our first true casualty when Sgt. Clyde Layton was killed by a mine explosion. While clearing a minefield, steel posts were driven into the ground along the perimeter of the cleared area, with white tape strung from post to post to mark the safe area. As Sergeant Layton's squad was clearing a German minefield, he carried a bundle of steel posts to the end of the cleared area and threw them to the ground. Sadly, the end of the bundle landed just beyond the safe area and detonated a mine, killing him instantly. It was a grim reminder of things to come.

The stress affected the men in many ways. It slowly eats away your well-being until something snaps. Our second casualty was unanticipated. One of our cooks, who never had to venture out of the building housing the kitchen, couldn't deal with the thought of being under surveillance by the Germans. Worrying about the possibility of being killed or wounded by mortar or artillery, he lost it one night. He broke down and cried like a baby, urinated and defecated in his clothes until he was carried away by the medics. He was reassigned to the rear echelon unit after treatment and recuperation, never to return to combat duty.

Each division engineer company had two bulldozers, a big D-8 diesel and a smaller R-4 gas dozer. The R-4 operator slept in the same building as I did and parked his dozer beside the building. After being under observation by the enemy and not being bothered by their artillery for almost a month, we began to get a little careless and reckless at times. While we could get away with quite a bit during the daylight hours, we did most of our work under the cover of darkness. To help waste time, I would climb up in the R-4, dig a hole, and fill it again. I enjoyed my little game until Captain Snow put an end to it by informing me that my bulldozer work might give the enemy the idea that something might be going on that was worthy of a few rounds of artillery. This ended my bulldozing career.

The Germans had in their arsenal an antipersonnel mine called the "S mine." It was filled with a one-fourth-inch diameter ball bearings and/or small pieces of what looked like chopped-up brake rods and was the work of the devil. When detonated, a projectile, flew about six feet into the air before it exploded, sending hundreds of ball bearing-like pieces in a 360-degree pattern. Statistics show us that "S mines" took 50% of our men out of combat and/or away from clearing a minefield.

They also had another anti-personnel mine, the Schu mine. It too was the work of the devil. It was made completely of wood with small brads holding it together & containing a ¼ pound block of TNT. The only metal was the shaft, making it next to impossible to detect. The lid rested on the butterfly pin of the igniter. When stepped on, the pin was removed, exploding the TNT. It was designed to blow off or mangle the foot of the victim who would need three or four men to care for a wounded man, where none were needed for a dead man.

We were eager to join up with the Anzio beachhead forces, which had endured much punishment and suffered many casualties, both killed and wounded. They had Germans on three sides and had their backs to the Tyrrhenian Sea (Wes Zylstra was there at Anzio) on the other. March 26, 1944, was a happy day when we pushed the enemy back far enough for them to leave the beachhead and join us later in the Eternal City, Rome. This was an exciting day for all of us! We had been hearing about Rome since we first went into the line, a goal we fought hard to reach. (Once again, Wes Zylstra was fighting his way into Rome with his company.)

The combat-weary men of the Fifth Army Infantry who had pursued the Germans across the Tiber River were the symbols of liberation. The people of Rome were overjoyed to see us! They lined the streets and cheered as we drove or marched by the crowds of liberated Italians. We had reserved a small cache of candies and cigarettes that we tossed as we passed. It was fun to see them fight and scramble for the prizes. Yet amidst all this excitement, tucked away in our minds, was the thought of the enemy we were chasing. Rome had been spared the damage inflicted on other cities.

We passed under the balcony from which Dictator Benito Mussolini delivered many of his speeches. One of our GIs climbed to the balcony and began to imitate Mussolini in an exaggerated way, using all the gestures the pompous dictator had used. The Italian people loved it! They laughed and applauded wildly, thoroughly enjoying it as it brought some long-overdue humor into their lives. The guy was a hero and even had his picture in papers, magazines, as well as Stars and Stripes. It was well worth the fifteen minutes of fame.

After passing through most of Rome, we stopped at the site of the Rome Summer Olympic Games. We felt privileged to be able to swim in the unheated Olympic-sized pool. Imagine the sight of 150 men without the benefit of a swimming suit. It was the first opportunity to take what resembled a bath. We always referred to the pool as a part of the Mussolini Military Academy. Then it was back to business as usual disarming booby traps, mines, and following the enemy.

As engineers, we were assigned the task of blazing a new road, trail, over the hills and through the forests that would accommodate the Army's four-wheel vehicles. After several days of falling trees, blowing stumps and rocks, using a lot of explosives, we all suffered headaches from breathing the fumes and smoke of the TNT. We worked around the clock to complete the job, but fortunately, we were able to capture and reopen the main highway once held by the Germans.

The weather had improved, the ground was pretty well dried out, and the roads didn't need our attention. We knew things were about to happen, but not when. A trip to the front on the night of May 11, 1944, we were driven most of the way to wherever we were going. There we received orders to clear a minefield, stressing the point that we *had* to finish the job and be out of there before 11:00 p.m. We were also to be alert for the possible German patrols in the area. This concept was frightening, but we were making good progress and finding mines. Suddenly, we heard a yell of pain and heard a parachute flare shooting skyward. It was my good friend and tent-mate, Courtland "Jumbo" Wright, who had stepped on and detonated a magnesium flare, which shot upward several hundred feet. Then it exploded and burst into a very bright light that lit up the whole area. It hung from a small parachute that seemed to take forever to hit the ground.

This meant two things. First, we all fell flat against the ground and lay motionless until the flare landed and extinguished. Second, we had to get out of there quick, as the Germans knew it had to be the enemy in their area. The Germans would blanket the area with artillery and mortar shells. Just as we were climbing onto the truck, we noticed it was 11:00 p.m. right on the dot. Every Allied artillery piece, infantry mortar, every gun on all Navy ships on both coasts of Italy opened fire on the Germans in an effort to weaken their defenses and destroy their bunkers. Through Allied aerial surveillance over the previous months, we knew the location of their artillery guns, supply depot, ammunition dumps, and buildings they had been using the last six months. All targets were barraged in order to force them to retreat from the high ground they held. Multiple tons of ammunition were thrown at them. It looked like the most spectacular July 4 celebration that one could ever imagine. This barrage went on for two days and three nights before the Allied infantry broke through enemy line.

Before this spring offensive, we received training in how to arm and fire the antitank bazookas. This weapon fired a rocket-type projectile that would burn a hole in the side of a tank. Hot molten metal sprayed the inside of the tank and caused death or severe burns to the occupants. Firing it was a two-man operation, one man to aim and another to load it. While loading the bazooka, we were taught to stand to one side or the other, but not directly behind it. Because, in the excitement and stress of the moment, the operator inadvertently touched the trigger while the rocket was being loaded, the rocket blast would kill the loader. The concussion and blast was awesome to behold! The reverse blast would knock down a propped-up board twenty-five feet away and capable of blowing off the head of the man right off his shoulders.

As the Germans retreated, we followed along behind. We were kept busy repairing roads and building bypasses where bridges had been blown. Sharp hairpin turns were blown by the enemy to stop the endless flow of Allied supplies and ammunition heading to the front. It was impossible to visualize the destruction that rained upon the German-occupied areas held during the past winter. Our artillery destroyed almost every building suspected of storing enemy supplies or personnel. The small town of Santa Maria was damaged to the point where we could hardly drive through because of the amount of rubble clogging the streets.

Hundreds of homes, buildings, and some small towns were completely devastated by our bombardment. Unfortunately, many Italian civilians living under German occupation were killed and their homes destroyed. After chasing the Germans out of the area, we were royally welcomed by the Italians. Thankful to see us and to show their gratitude, they very generously offered gifts of whatever little they had, whether it was a loaf of bread, eggs, fruit, wine or pasta.

This was the Eighty-eighth Division's first taste of offensive combat. We were the first all selective service personnel to go into combat. That fact may have lulled the Germans into thinking we couldn't possibly know how to fight and they were completely surprised to know we were a draftee division. The captured enemy testified about the ferocity of our fighting. Up until this time, the Eighty-eighth was known as the Ranger Division, but the prisoners thought we fought like devils. Referring to our blue division insignia shoulder patches and on our helmets in the form of a blue four-leaf clover, we were nicknamed the Blue Devils. We were known from then on as the Blue Devil Division.

Twenty-three days after the "push" began, Lieutenant Dykers "Doc" stopped by my company area for a visit. He was exhausted, appeared very gaunt, and had lost weight. When the infantry has the enemy on the run, you keep pushing. He hadn't had a cooked meal, a decent night of sleep, or even a hot cup of coffee in all that time, only rations and catnaps. Doc had been shot through the hand by a machine gun bullet and was on his way back from the front lines to a hospital for treatment and R & R. It was almost a year before we saw one another again. When seen again, Doc had survived the battle for Mt. Battaglia, been wounded severely, lost a lot of his hearing, and re-classified as unfit for combat.

Returning from the front lines was always stressful. We didn't realize just how deeply it had affected us and the toll it had taken. After a few days, we found ourselves relaxing and enjoying life. No listening for artillery and mortars, no worrying about mines or snipers. When returning to combat, the stress began again as soon as we stepped up to the truck. We knew where we were going and what lay ahead. Our pride wouldn't let us do otherwise. Everyone else felt exactly like you did, and there's nothing we could do about it anyway. The closer we got to the front, the more stressed we became. When we saw or heard the first incoming shell land, our stress levels hit the top. After living under these conditions for so long, we simply had to adapt and go about our jobs. By now, I had become responsible for a squad of twelve men, and that was scary.

Crossing the Rapido River had been a fiasco. This time we had all the ingredients for a recipe for distress, the probability of crossing the Arno River, located south of Florence. After we had successfully pushed the Germans across that river, we passed through a forest where we saw huge trees almost transformed into kindling. The intense artillery blasts leveled that area. The sight was both awesome and sobering when we stopped a few miles south of Mt. Grande.

The United States granted the American GIs the privilege of voting. It was here that many of us voted for the first time in a general election. President Franklin Delanor Roosevelt was elected for an unprecedented third term. By now the cold weather had set in, and we were issued mummy-type sleeping bags. While the enlisted men had to turn in a blanket, the officers were allowed to have a sleeping bag and keep their previously issued blankets.

It was now November. One cold, rainy night, a bunch of replacement infantrymen bivouacked across the gully from us. They were as green as grass as far as fighting was concerned. Some of them made a huge mistake by leaving a lot of gear they would need later at the front. I walked over to check the plunder they had left behind the next morning. I quickly picked up twelve wet wool blankets; even a wet blanket will keep you warm if you have nothing else. Through a great deal of effort and argument with the supply sergeant, I was able to convince him that my guys were entitled to keep the two blankets we had. We tried to exchange the shoes for better-fitting ones, but that wasn't possible.

Because the rain made fields and some roads impassable, the front lines stopped for the winter. Our main chore was maintaining and keeping the same roads open. It was a wet and cold winter, and our pup tents were definitely not insulated. I dug an extra wide foxhole back into a bank and erected my tent over it, giving me protection on three sides from the enemy artillery and allowing room enough for me to sit up. The first night it was so wet my sleeping bag was soaked. Then I dug a shallow ditch down the middle of my dirt tent floor, directing the water out, placed some boards over it, sleeping over my own private creek, which only proved that I could sleep anytime and anywhere, and we continued to work in mud and rain on a daily basis.

Each time we were relieved for some R & R, we went back into the line in another area, relieving another engineer unit. One time we inherited a section of road where there was no gravel available. Even though the road ran parallel to a gravel-bottomed river, the "brass" opted to use rock hauled from a quarry and spread on the roads where we had the "privilege" of breaking it into smaller pieces with sledgehammers. Every day we hit the road, literally, at eight o'clock in the morning, had hot chow at noon. We didn't head back until five o'clock just like a road gang of convicts. We soon learned rock has a grain just as wood does. It wasn't how, but where you hit it.

In addition to the noise of trucks dumping rock, jeeps going by, the pounding of hammers breaking rock, we had to stay alert for the sound of enemy artillery in the area. The Germans must have had a gun trained on the road because they shelled it every day. Our men were wounded, and others went stark raving mad from the stress. It was the humorless who cracked under the strain. The medic attached to our unit was hard drinking, hard fighting on R & R, but sober as a judge in combat. He never cracked under the strain and often worked right along beside us until the German guns went off. One thing was certain, if you dove into a ditch, you always came out muddy or bloody from head to toe.

One day the infamous German gun sounded; I remember crawling under a stair landing, looking around in the house of refuge. I urged

Dan Donavon to join me. Just as a shell landed near the door, the noise was deafening. Dan's protruding knee was slashed by debris. The jeep carrying two men pulled up seeking safety; they never had a chance. One had the top of his head sliced off and the other was pinned to the seat by a huge piece of shrapnel. Both died on the spot. The jeep blocked several trucks in the procession, leaving them all vulnerable to shelling. One of my men, Pvt. Andy Murdaugh, took charge at the risk of his own life to get the driver to move the truck and clear up a dangerous situation under the circumstances for which I recommended him for the Silver Star.

I was assigned to attend a mine and demolition school located near the city of Caserta, just north of Naples. While I was gone to school, the rest of the battalion was given ten days of R & R. When we returned to the front, we moved into an area where an artillery battalion had been bivouacked for quite some time. They were quite creative in that they used wooden shipping boxes used to ship and move powder, projectiles or shell casings to build a number of small two-man huts. Each one was complete with two bunks along one end and with outside walls sandbagged for protection from shrapnel, but leaving the roof vulnerable and unprotected. They also filled hundreds of the cardboard tubes with dirt or gravel, laid them horizontally, using dirt for mortar, to form wind—and almost-shrapnel-proof walls for a building large enough to use as a hall capable of feeding 150 men. The ends were built to accommodate a gabled roof covered with canvas. Who knows where they scrounged the canvas! Since it was built on a slope, one end was about ten feet high compared to seven on the other. Our kitchen crew moved their equipment inside. This was the first time we were able to eat our meals in a dry, protected place out of the weather. It was heated by the stoves and ovens used to prepare our food, warm and dry our clothes. We were even able to watch a couple movies, but we were well aware of the threat of artillery fire and the non-protective canvas roof where the holes were stark reminders of its inability to protect us.

There was a huge cave nearby in which they had built enough wooden bunk bed frames to accommodate quite a number of men. Unfortunately, this was a dangerous place to be when the Germans had large artillery shells that were capable of reaching that distance. Case in point, as I entered the company area the day I returned from mine and demolition school, one of those "booster shells" malfunctioned by exploding the complete shell over our head. The shrapnel killed several men and wounded several others, including my friend, Courtland "Jumbo" Wright, with whom I had been talking when it exploded. He had been leaning over his steel helmet washing and shaving when the shrapnel cut a deep gash in his right shoulder muscle, and another narrowly missed his genitals as another piece tore through his right pant leg. He was sent back to the hospital for stitches and recuperation.

The leather shoes we were issued, unfortunately they soaked up water like a sponge, and there was not a place to dry them; consequently, we had wet feet much of the time. With the advent of fall and winter seasons and the wet weather accompanying them, we never had a dry pair of shoes or socks. A large number of the men lost their toes due to constant dampness, cold feet, and poor circulation known as trench foot when they turned black.

The Army responded by issuing every man two pairs of boots made with rubber bottoms and leather tops. They came with three thick felt insoles and three pairs of thick wool socks. With these safeguards, every man was charged with the responsibility to rotate the felt pads each day, keeping a dry one next to his feet. We were required to wear two pairs of socks, rotating them and keeping them dry next to our feet. To ensure dry feet and no trench foot, every squad sergeant was required to make a daily pickup of a dirty pair of socks from each of his men, turn them in for washing, and receive a clean pair in exchange to give to his men. Now it was a court-martial offense if a GI developed trench foot.

It was natural to expect that some men under the extreme stress risk their lives to escape the hell they were living in. They chose to live with the blight of a court-martial on their record and be sentenced to time in the division stockade.

The Division Commander, Major General John Sloan, moved the Division Stockade up to an area right behind the front lines of combat. Under these conditions, all stockade prisoners were surrounded by a barbed wire enclosure, living in a pup tent-covered foxhole, and had nowhere to run when enemy shell fire was dropped in this area. The MPs guarding the prisoners were living out the sentences imposed on the prisoners. Prisoners and their guards were picked up by the engineers to help work on the roads in the morning. Their guards accompanied them to ensure they didn't escape and guaranteed their return at the end of the day. If a prisoner escaped, the guard would be subject to complete the prisoner's sentence.

The Germans seemed to know when we were going, so we drew artillery fire often. Their 88mm guns were tremendously effective high-velocity weapons that seemed to shoot flat trajectory shots. If you heard the shell coming, it was already too late. That sound was the most terrifying sound of the war! I had developed a horrible fear of being buried in Italy.

Each time we moved to a new area during the winter months in support of the front lines, we each had to prepare our own place to live and sleep when not working. All our food was prepared in the kitchen mounted on a truck, but the food was served outside regardless of the weather, without a tarp over the serving line. Going through the chow line filling our mess kits, we ate our meals in the rain, snow, and mud while seated on our steel helmets. At one point the Germans had been retreating so fast, we lived on K rations for several weeks. Whenever a pigeon, small flock of chickens, or a wild turkey blessed us with their presence, they were cordially invited for dinner.

One of the most frightening and heart-wrenching things I think I ever witnessed occurred during and following a devastating and deadly artillery barrage. Because of blocked roads, we had just arrived in this new area after hiking the whole day. The enemy's timing couldn't have been worse for us. We had a lot of men milling around in the open. Suddenly, the sky was raining artillery shells, with explosions everywhere. Our men scrambled for cover in ditches, behind logs, rocks, and under tanks. When it was over, the dead and wounded were everywhere. I dove with others under a tank where we were protected by its tracks, but the man in front had the top of his head cut off as slick and clean as cutting a watermelon. We knew enough to run for cover, but the mule train carrying supplies to the area was decimated. Some mules just stood there being killed outright, while others were wounded and had to be shot.

As we lay there and looked at the havoc surrounding us, we watched as a mule skinner dutifully approached a badly wounded mule, took out his .45-caliber automatic, made a cross between the eyes and ears of the mule, placed his pistol against its head, and shot it. Its front knees buckled for a moment, shook its head from side to side; then it stood straight again. The poor mule skinner repeated this until he had shot the mule seven times before it stayed down and died. It was an awful thing for us to watch, but the mule skinner was doing what he was taught.

We were in no-man's-land, between our front line troops and the enemy, with infantry around us for security. We had to concentrate on detecting mines and be alert for enemy action at the same time. If you missed a mine and stepped on it, you were history. I was still responsible for my twelve men, which added to my personal stress level. When metal detectors were first issued, they came equipped with an audio resonator attached to the shoulder strap near your ear. When passed over metal, sound emitted through the resonator, telling you metal was present. The problem was the sound was loud enough for the enemy to hear us, we thought. Soon the resonators where replaced with headphones, and then we couldn't hear the enemy.

As spring of 1945 approached, the roads and fields dried and firmed up and another offensive action began. The constant bombing and strafing over the winter months by the Allies was pretty effective. The Po River Valley, a long sought-after Allied target, was almost within sight. At one point, my squad was attached to a small special task force formed for a special mission. As we waited, occasional artillery and mortar shells landed in the area. Suddenly, among these sounds, we heard the muffled sound of a mine exploding. Experience tells you a man was injured or killed. We ran as we knew someone was hurt.

On arrival we saw a number of infantrymen gathering to help their injured buddy. A jeep had run over a mine and been destroyed, and the driver lay severely injured nearby. I voted to wait for a medic; but they quickly brought another jeep, loaded some bundles of grain for a cushion, and loaded the injured driver aboard. A buddy jumped into the front seat and two more sat beside their injured buddy in the back. They didn't drive three feet before they hit another mine. Now there were five men injured or killed. I had just turned to the right as the concussion of the explosion knocked me to the ground. I heard a dull thump near my feet and recognized it to be the body of the first injured driver. His carotid artery had been severed as his life's blood was being pumped away with every heartbeat. Given a shot of morphine by the medic, the driver was left to die in my arms.

I hadn't realized that I had been wounded until I went to the aid station to wash my face and hands. I was a bloody mess, having sixty-five holes in my face and hands. A man from my engineer company lost an eye, another a puncture wound below his navel. When the medic swabbed the wounds with methylate and applied a big white bandage to my face and arm. His services were accompanied with a heated lecture from S. Sgt. Bodie, only because he loved us. When we arrived back at the company area, I immediately wrote my parents to assure them of my good health before they received a telegram from the War Department. Unfortunately, every letter we wrote was censored by the company officers, lest we gave away information to the enemy.

That night, forty-eight hours after being wounded, we again had to work under cover of darkness to clear a road littered with mines. It was a beautiful moonlit night, too bright for our comfort. We felt the Germans could see us and the carnage of the previous battle. Bodies and damaged equipment were scattered along the road. When you carried a cartridge belt filled with ammo, a bayonet, and a canteen filled with water attached day after day, it gets heavy. I had often seen infantrymen with government-issued suspenders for their cartridge belts. We wished we had them too. I quietly removed a pair from one of the dead bodies, complete with his trench knife. Those suspenders were a godsend. I still have the trench knife, which is one of the few souvenirs that I brought home with me.

I felt that the big white bandage was a neon sign reflecting in the moonlight, so I tore it off. By this time my face was beginning to throb with pain. I can still remember the stench as I pulled the biggest wound open and released the rotting matter inside. The wound became infected from the embedded dirt that had not been removed by the doctor. So they sent me along with the other wounded by ambulance for a ten-day stay at a convalescent hospital. The newfound quiet away from the front line took some adjustment. I also had some dental work done there.

The passages from my nose to my ear were plugged, which was the reason for my earaches. So the doctor ran a rubber tube from my ear to his and then inserted up my nose what appeared to be a long bent hollow needle with a threaded fitting on one end. I couldn't believe how far he pushed that thing up my nose! I was thinking it would hit the top of my head. When it was in place, he threaded a syringe onto it and began pumping air. As the pressure mounted, the pain increased. I had never felt anything so painful. I thought my head would split right down the middle. Tears ran freely because of the pressure on the tear ducts, until there was a dull sound of release, opening the plugged passageway. It felt like being in a Boeing wind test tunnel. I had no idea how long it had been plugged or where it went, but that was the last of my earaches.

I still remember the beautiful summer day I returned to my squad. Company A was set up in an orchard where the peaches were tree ripened, just hanging, waiting to be picked. My buddy and I picked a shelter half with peaches, grabbed it by the four corners, and carried it back to our platoon. The peaches were so juicy and ripe that we dipped the juice with our canteen cups and drank it. I've never tasted such delicious and sweet peaches. Now I had to get acclimated into the combat mode again after ten days of quiet and peace.

By this time the Germans were in full retreat, and we chased them relentlessly until we reached the Po River with its blown bridges. Beaten thoroughly, hungry, and exhausted, they surrendered by the thousands. They were so tired of war, retreating, and the suffering from the humiliation of surrender. A company of the 313th Engineers was assigned the duty of guarding a prisoner of war cage by using a former stockyard. As they came walking in, they were directed to the various pens while waiting to be transported to a huge POW camp near Verona. As fast as one truck was loaded and dispatched, another sixty or more prisoners, all standing, were loaded up. An unbelievable sight awaited us when we actually reached the Po River. The blown bridges cut off their escape route, leaving thousand pieces of their equipment.

The blown bridges also meant we were temporarily stalled until a pontoon bridge could be built. Truck, cars, tanks, half tracks, artillery pieces, mobile ordinance shops with all the tools, and hundreds of horses they had confiscated from the Italians to pull their equipment these last few miles. After all the fighting we had experienced together, our officers were kind enough to give us free time as we waited for the completion of the bridge. Here it was in the middle of April 1945, with beautiful weather, free to wander through the German equipment for souvenirs. One of the most prized souvenirs was a German Luger pistol, or a P-38 pistol which the officers usually carried. I eventually found one for myself.

A number of our men hailed from Texas and Oklahoma, and others had a yen for being cowboys. The next days were filled with horse races, roping, relay races, and scaled-down rodeo acts. It was a wonderful way for our men and the Italians to release stress and the horrors of the past year. Many of the Italians were profusely grateful to us for their liberation. Out of their meager supplies, they offered to prepare meals as a token of their appreciation.

Poverty was rampant. Their clothes worn bare and then patched several times. A scene that still haunts me today was to see a woman and her children standing in line with their little pails and kettles to receive whatever was left in our mess kits following our meals. We often saw the hurt and humiliation in their eyes as they had to put their pride in their pockets and stoop to begging for the scraps from our plates to feed their families. Many cans of food and loaves of bread were liberated from our kitchen and given to these poor people.

After days of play and waiting for the bridge to be completed, we crossed the Po River and drove all night. We finally arrived at a very small town where their stone bridge had been destroyed. We were told to rest up as Bailey bridge equipment was on the way and we would be working hard the next day. Our prayers had been answered! Our company commander, Captain Joseph Johnson, was standing on the opposite side of the blown bridge, yelling to inform us, "All German forces in Italy have surrendered!" I don't know what I had expected to happen when the war ended. It was so sudden, so quiet, and yet so memorable to think back on. We had lived through hell, seen many of our buddies killed or injured, worked, walked, ate, and slept in mud and survived.

Our happiness was short-lived, however, as one German division commander refused to surrender. We had chased him deep into the Italian Alps. I couldn't help thinking that I might be killed by some Nazi after the war was over. We were overcome by very strange feelings of insecurity and vulnerability as we drove through thousands of fully armed German soldiers as we returned to our company area. All were staring at us, the members of a nonprofessional all Draftee Division wearing the blue clover leaf insignia on our helmets and shoulders. Described by the enemy as the Fighting Blue Devils, these same men whipped their butts and pushed them all the way from Africa, Sicily, Salerno, Anzio, and Naples to the Italian Alps.

I firmly believe any man serving in a front line unit who lived through the war cannot deny the grace of God as He protects us in so many instances. Today it makes me shudder when I recall just one of these times. We were on R & R in the Voltaire area. Lee Wisdom,

Paul Hackler, a truck driver, and I were sent to collect German land mines that had been cleared from a road. They were to be used for training in laying a minefield and sweeping or detecting mines while using a metal detector. When we reached a pile of mines, we threw them onto the metal bed of the truck as if they were blocks of wood then walked over them while moving to the next pile. This process was repeated over and over until we had enough. Then they bounced around during the bumpy ride back. Only God's grace prevented them from exploding.

On the morning of August 9, 1945, we were trucked to Livorno (Leghorn) and loaded aboard ship. It was a rather somber group as we anticipated a long boat ride to an unknown destination. Sailing on the eleventh, I remember stopping off the island of Gibraltar for a brief time, supposedly to receive further orders. The war with Japan ended August 14, 1945, at 6:00 a.m.

August 18, we were awakened by the announcement "This ship has been diverted from Manila, the Philippines, to Boston, Massachusetts, USA!" Outside of one long cheer, not much was said when we learned that the war had ended. We were going home at last. We docked in Boston Harbor, August 22, amid a crowd of cheering, smiling people who applauded us as we walked down the gangplank onto the pier. We were served cakes, cookies, milk, coffee, and fresh fruits. Even the ships in Boston Harbor greeted us by blowing their whistles and horns. The decks were lined with returning GIs; the conquering heroes were home! While this was very exciting, it seemed to take forever to get our ship next to the pier and get the gangplank in place.

After walking down the gangplank and being served the delicious goodies, we marched aboard a passenger train waiting to deliver us to Camp Miles Standish, Massachusetts. Not knowing what was expected of us, we were marched to the Base Theater and given a lecture on what facilities were available, their expectations, and that we would be sent home as soon as travel arrangements could be made. I stood in line for two hours waiting for my turn, calling Ardie at work in Mt. Vernon and my folks in Oak Harbor, letting them know I was back in the States. We were put on a train five days later that took us south through Rhode Island and Connecticut to New York City. From there we traveled north through Buffalo, then south and west through Pennsylvania, Ohio, Illinois, Missouri, Kansas, Colorado, Utah, Idaho, Oregon, and finally, Washington. Being August, the grasses were dry and the grain fields were a beautiful gold. The best part of this trip was seeing the beauty of the countryside passing through the small towns and large cities.

I was looking forward to the day when Ardie and I would be married during those five days of travel by train. We arrived in Tacoma and were trucked to Fort Lewis where we were processed and allowed to go to our homes. Arriving at the Seattle Greyhound bus depot at Eighth and Stewart, I met and rode with Bob Mesman of Oak Harbor Transfer to Everett where he lived. I hitch-hiked and caught a ride to Mt. Vernon. Thinking it was too late to call Ardie, I walked the streets and met a guy who had caught an earlier bus. Together we walked the streets, drank coffee, and visited the night watchman at the Carnation Dairy plant until we felt we could call our folks. I called Ardie.

We planned our wedding for the following weekend, September 7, following a week-long honeymoon. I gladly reported for my discharge, which took longer because I had been on furlough. October 21, 1945, was the day I had looked forward to since February 12, 1943. With the huge influx of construction people and Navy personnel into little Oak Harbor, and with no housing available, we lived with my parents for almost two months. I had my girl by my side, and we loved being with my family, but we were overjoyed to be able to eventually establish our own home after waiting five years and two months since our first date.

Ardie and I have three wonderful children, seven grandchildren, who have continued to love us in spite of the mistakes we made, and recently we have celebrated our sixty-fourth anniversary. God loves me the way that I am, but he loves me too much to leave me that way. Sometimes I look back over the eighty-seven years God has given me and marvel at the patience of this wonderful Lord I serve and the miracles of my survival during years in Italy.

HANK'S STORY

Guest author:

Christopher Saxman

Henry "Hank" Koetje US Army
66th Black Panther Infantry Division
1943-1946

Introduction

Hank Koetje served his country simply because his country asked him to. He left home as a young man of nineteen—a boy really—who had rarely left his hometown and went to war in Europe, a war that was producing many casualties and deaths. He knew he was facing death, he knew he may not come home, but he went anyway. He went because he had a sense of duty, yes. He went because it was the right thing to do, yes. But mostly, he went because he was needed. His country needed him. Hank did face death and he prevailed, and he prevailed with valor. It is the men like Hank Koetje whom we have to thank for this country.

After returning home, Hank continued to build his country, starting and nurturing several important businesses, businesses without which his community could not have grown into the community it became. Hank is a quiet, modest man, a proud man, and he has a lot to be proud of.

As a further note, I must say, it was I who sought Hank out for this writing, not he who was looking to tell his story.

Contents

Chapter 1: Small Town Boy 193

Chapter 2: In the Army Now 197

Chapter 3: Reassigned 201

Chapter 4: Off to Europe 203

Chapter 5: Torpedoed 206

Chapter 6: Sent to the Front 210

Chapter 7: After the Fighting 216

Chapter 8: The Rest of the Story 219

Chapter 1

Small Town Boy

It's been a long life, a good life rich with a variety of experiences. A man can't ask for too much more than that. I was born on Whidbey Island in Puget Sound, in the small town of Oak Harbor some eighty-four years ago as of this writing. I had a wonderful childhood, playing in the freedom of outdoors, often along the water. My family life was good, just as it should be, and I was close to my mom, Hattie, and my dad, Ben Koetje. He had moved to Whidbey from McBain, Michigan, in 1905. On the island there were lots of Dutch families who had much in common, and ours fit right in. In 1920, Dad met my mom, Hatti Meeter, who was from South Holland, Illinois. They married, and along came me with my two brothers and two sisters.

Of course, we didn't travel too much in those days, but I did get to make a few trips into Seattle, which, for us, was a big deal. Then in 1932, when I was nine years old, my family, my uncle Tom, Aunt Grace, and I took a vacation back to Michigan. All of us went except for my baby brother Al, who did not come along. My dad drove us in the family car, a 1929 Studebaker. My dad had built cabinets along the running boards, so we had lots of storage space for the six of us. We went to see family there, and it was a great trip. It took five days just to drive the distance, but it was fun to see some of the rest of the world. We went through Yellowstone Park and saw the sights there. We even had bears get into our food. This was my only worldly experience until I was drafted.

My dad was a big, strong, hardworking guy. He managed the local lumber company, Columbia Lumber. The business was located along the water near downtown Oak Harbor, and they supplied lumber for the north end of the island. Lumber was brought in by boat or barge to their dock. Dad was proud to have been the first fire Chief of Oak Harbor and one of the founding members of the Oak Harbor Rotary Club, 1936. I got into Rotary early; I was the first student Rotarian from Oak Harbor High. Might have had something to do with my dad being a founding member, but I was a good student and a pretty good representative of the student body. The program is still in operation to this day.

I went to school in Oak Harbor, and I was a good student, getting mostly Bs. My real love, however, was sports. I played football, baseball, and basketball; but baseball was my favorite. I played first base as I admired Lou Gehrig a lot. He could do it all. I played other positions as well, but first base was my favorite. We played towns from all over the area like Edison, Coupeville, Point Townsend, Burlington, Langley, Mt. Vernon, and Anacortes; so we did quite a bit of traveling in the local area. I enjoyed the trips, but I liked being at home.

For a couple of years we had a pretty good basketball team, winning nineteen and losing only two. One year we played the much larger O'Day from Seattle. They were a real powerhouse, but on that day we gave them a run for their money and ultimately won the game. We even made the Seattle P-I about how we upset O'Day. It was the talk of the town back in Oak Harbor, and we were heroes for a week or so.

**The 1941 Oak Harbor championship Basketball team.
Hank can be seen in the middle row far right.**

I graduated from Oak Harbor High in 1941. We had a ceremony at school, at which Senator Pearl Wanamaker spoke, but our class had only thirty-six members. I went to work for my dad in the lumberyard over the summer then went on to the University of Washington in the fall. The next summer I went back to work at Columbia Lumber. With all the construction revving up on the Navy base, the demand for lumber was way up. Lots of lumber and supplies were coming into the yard by barge and boat. With the war breaking out, I knew it would only be a matter of time until I was drafted, so in the fall I did not go back to the U; I kept working. The whole town was booming at that time, and work was good. Everyone had money in their pockets.

While working in the yard, I made friends with Mr. Gene Dunlap, of Dunlap Towing of LaConner. They barged in most of our inventory at the yard, and he owned the towing company. He also was captain on one of the boats. We would talk when he came in, and he took a liking to me. He was a very nice, down-to-earth person. One day he offered me a job. He had received a contract from the Navy to keep Crescent Harbor clear of drifting logs. This was important because the seaplanes were continually landing and taking off there. The PBYs were thin-skinned and no match for a big Doug fir. He needed a responsible boat captain and offered me my own boat. I took the job.

My boat was a tug, the *Lilly*. Small but maneuverable, she was great. I had two men who worked on the boat with me. We worked all hours of the day and often at night to keep the harbor clear. A couple of times Navy boats ran aground on a sandbar, and we had to come to the rescue and pull them off. I really enjoyed that work; it was the best job ever.

After a little over a year as tug captain, I received my draft notice; I was to join the Army. I knew it was coming and was just waiting to do my duty. First thing was the physical. I was concerned that the asthma I had would keep me out. My plan was to keep quiet, but I worried they would find out and 4-F me. We would listen to the war news every evening on the radio. Everyone was behind the war, and I really wanted to do my part.

March of 1943, at nineteen, I said good-bye to my family and boarded the bus. I looked out the window and could see my mom crying. We were pretty close. There had been lots of bad news on the war front and lots of men were dying, and now her boy was going off to who knows what fate. We picked up several other draftees along the way, stopping at Coupeville and Langley. The bus took us to the ferry, and we walked on. At the other side, we were picked up by an Army bus. Of course, this was well before any freeway. The bus took Highway 99 to downtown Seattle and again stopped to pick up several other inductees along the way. I was starting out on a new adventure. I was looking forward, but at the same time, there was some apprehension. It felt good that I wasn't alone.

Chapter 2

In the Army Now

I really didn't know what to expect on arrival in Seattle. As soon as we got there, they put us on another Army bus, and we took off for Fort Lewis. They cut our hair off and issued us uniforms and duffel bags to keep all our stuff in. We waited around for a couple of days until there were lots of recruits in the barracks. They then put us all on a troop train to Fort Warden in Cheyenne, Wyoming. As the train clicked along the tracks, I watched the countryside go by and thought about what might be in store for me. I really didn't know what to expect; it was all new.

Didn't take too long before I started to feel homesick, but I was in the Army now, and there was no going back. At Fort Warden we had basic training, what now is called boot camp. We did a lot of running and exercises, but we also had classes and some training. The classes were for the Quartermasters Corps, provisions, and supply. I was also trained in vehicle maintenance. We spent time marching and learning to shoot, lots of practice shooting at a silhouette of a man. We weren't allowed off the base for three months.

Our lieutenant who often drilled us was from Brooklyn, New York. Being from the Northwest, I had never heard an accent like that, and he made quite an impression on me. After giving an order to police the area, clean up, he would shout, "All I wanna see is asses and elbows!" He often used another expression that really showed his accent: "Yous better wourk hard or there's no tourky on Toisday."

I was assigned to the Quartermasters Corps in Cheyenne and went to a regular unit, but shortly thereafter, I got new orders. Looking ahead to the end of the war, the Army figured it was going to need a lot of engineers to help rebuild Europe. They picked out two thousand men to put through engineering school for this task. They were sent to universities across the country, and I was to be one of those men. My orders were to report to the University of Wyoming in Laramie as a part of the ASTP program. Two hundred others were sent to Laramie along with me.

I spent the next year and a half in engineering school there in Laramie. I shared a dorm room with one other Army fellow. It was pretty much like going to college, except we wore our uniforms every day as a part of the regular Army. We had classes with the regular student body, but also we met as an Army unit. Sometimes for meetings, and other times simply to pick up our area. We also met at the gym every day for calisthenics to keep us in shape, and it worked. I enjoyed the engineering courses and did well. We had to take trigonometry and calculus, but I found them challenging.

We got only one day a week off, from six on Saturday until six on Sunday. That gave us enough time to go into town, have a beer, and when we could find one, dance with a girl. Met a very nice girl there one evening with name of Florence. I liked to dance, so Florence and I did a lot of dancing, mostly to country music. It was Wyoming after all. She invited me on a couple of picnics with her family, and there were some other dates, but it was not all that serious.

The university had a very successful sports program. They were national basketball champs for their division the year before I arrived. I practiced with the team and even got in a couple of games for the Cowboys. That felt like a real accomplishment since they were so good. A kid from Oak Harbor playing for the national champions.

Weather in Laramie was good, though cold in the winter. We had lots of sun compared to Whidbey. One of the hotels even used it for advertising. They said that if the sun didn't shine that day, they would give you a free room. The altitude was at about 7,200 feet, and it was dry. I noticed that my asthma hadn't acted up in months, the climate I guess. It was a good life there at the U, and I enjoyed it.

I wrote often to my family back on Whidbey, and Mom wrote to me often with news from home. After the start of my second year, my dad made another trip back to Michigan to get a car he had purchased. On his way home he came through Laramie and stopped to see me. It sure was good to see him after more than a year. When he departed, he took the train and left the car with me. Wow, I had my own car!

Later in April, I got leave and drove the car home. This wasn't a sightseeing trip, however; I drove straight through, stopping only for gas and food. This is back before freeways, so the roads were two lanes with lots of traffic, and I wandered through every town between Laramie and Whidbey. Driving was work, but it was fun for me, and I felt real independent. By the time I got to Seattle, I could hardly keep my eyes open. I saw a sailor hitchhiking. I stopped and asked if he could drive, and he said yes, and he was going to Whidbey. I got in the back and was out like a light. Good thing he was honest. I could have ended up anywhere; I was so tired. He got me to Whidbey, and we said our good-byes.

Hank and his Mom before leaving for Europe and the front

It was so great to see my family, especially my mom. She was real happy I was home, even if for only a few days. While there, I met a girl by the name of Elaine. We saw a lot of each other and got kinda attached. We agreed that we would write to each other after I left.

Not long after I returned to Laramie, I got new orders. The Army had decided that, with the way the war was going, they needed soldiers more than they needed engineers. As a result, they snatched us out of the university and assigned us to an infantry unit. It was good while it lasted. The orders came down quickly, and we were on our way within the week.

Chapter 3

Reassigned

I was assigned to the Sixty-sixth Black Panther Infantry Division located in Little Rock, Arkansas. A troop train full of GIs took us to the base. It was a long ride, three days and two nights. We did have sleeping quarters, which were very utilitarian (converted Pullman cars), and we were stacked three high. There was a cafeteria on board, and that served us two meals a day. It was more or less like a chow hall. A line would form, and we'd take a plate to be loaded up with food, and then take it back to our seat to eat.

We received infantry training in Little Rock, but within thirty days we got new orders and were sent to Camp Rucker in Dothan, Alabama, for more training. We did lots of exercises, and at night when it was cool, we would go on long marches, sometimes thirty miles. We had lots of target practice with our rifles and even practiced with the bayonet mounted on the end of our rifles, in the event we were in hand-to-hand combat. This was getting real. I thought this place was a hellhole, but I was mistaken—that was still to come.

The humidity, heat, and exercise caused my asthma to flare up, and I had several occasions when it was hard to catch my breath. As a result, I was sent to the infirmary several times. The Army became aware of this and told me they were going to start proceedings to discharge me. I was a sergeant by this time, and I didn't want to be put out to pasture. They scheduled a hearing, and I was to appear before this medical evaluation board. Just before I was to be there, I took a really hot, steamy shower, figuring that would last me a couple of hours. I did manage to convince them it was nothing serious, and they sent me back to my unit.

When it became time for specific job assignments, I was sent to the weapons platoon as a mortar-man. We had to learn to fire the mortar and how to dial it in so we could hit the spot we were aiming for. We practiced a lot, and my squad got pretty sharp. My time there only lasted six months, thank goodness.

During my time at Camp Rucker, I was given two weeks' leave. I knew this would be my last leave before going to Europe and the fighting, so I jumped at the chance. I hopped a train to Chicago and there went to the airport for my first plane ride. I was excited, although a bit nervous. Once we were airborne, it was great, especially to see everything from the air. We flew through the Rocky Mountains and then the Cascades, what a sight! I was glued to the window. The flight took twelve hours and stopped twice, but it was much better and faster than any alternative and with our uniforms on, we were sent to the head of the line and got right on. People understood the contribution we were making in the war, and no one ever complained. After a very nice visit with my family, I returned to Camp Rucker by train.

It was time to get back to more training, and with the news we were getting from the front, we took our training seriously. We did get a couple of hours off on Saturday night. Time enough for a dinner or movie in town. I didn't party or even make too many friends during that time. We had a single purpose, and we knew what was ahead. It wasn't long until I got orders to report to New York City. The time was here to be shipped to the front.

Chapter 4

Off to Europe

We left Dothan, Alabama, on a troop train bound for New York City. It was about a two-day ride. On arrival, we were marched to the waterfront, where we organized and prepared to board a ship. November 15 they marched us up the gangplank to the troopship *George Washington*. We were finally told on board that we were bound for South Hampton, England. We were on our way to the war.

There were eight thousand of us, and it was a pretty tight fit. The bunks were stacked five high, and there was a continuous chow line. Again we were getting two meals a day. Many of the men suffered from seasickness, so if you were on a lower bunk, you had to watch out. There was a lot of poker-playing to pass the time.

Our ship was actually in a large convoy of ships, and we had several Navy destroyers as escort. In order to keep us from being torpedoed by a Nazi sub, the ship was moving in a zigzag pattern and continuously setting off depth charges. This was

Hank ready to ship overseas 1944

our first indication that we were really in the war. It made us all think. Under normal circumstances, the crossing took seven days, but because of the protective maneuvers, the trip took us fifteen days.

December 1, 1944, we landed in South Hampton, England. It had been a long trip from Alabama, especially for a boy from Oak Harbor, Washington. In South Hampton, we were sent to a bivouac area for staging. We were in large green canvas tents with perhaps twenty other soldiers. We were to organize and gather strength before the crossing to France and the front. In the three weeks I spent there, they did give us some liberty. Of course, we made a beeline for town, Dorchester, where we might find some entertainment, and we did. There were some pubs with beer and some live music. I even managed to get in a couple of dances with some English gals. It was a good relief from our worries about the front.

On Christmas Eve, December 24, they decided to treat us to a traditional turkey dinner. Cooks prepared turkeys, mashed potatoes, vegetables, cranberry sauce—the whole shooting match for all eight thousand of us. They put the dinners out, and we were about to sit down when an announcement came over the PA system. We were ordered to report to the dock immediately. We were forced to leave those beautiful dinners they had worked so hard to prepare sitting on the table. We were hurried to the dock, and then in a true Army "Hurry up and wait," we sat on the dock for twelve hours, waiting to board the ship.

Guys were getting more serious, so as a result, there was very little grab ass as we used to call it. Finally, word came down, and we started to board. Two thousand two hundred of us were to board the Belgian troopship *Leopoldville*. Up the gangplank with our weapons and duffel bags we went. It took us only a couple of hours to get aboard. It was early morning when we pulled anchor and set sail for France and the front. The D-day invasion had taken place several months before, on June 6, so by this time, we had a good foothold in France. We were assigned areas of the ship, and we settled in for the ride.

The ship traveled in a convoy again, with other troopships and several British destroyers escorting us. We made a turn and began crossing the channel. It was cold, and the wind was blowing pretty well. As a result, the seas were heavy and the ship was rolling to and fro. It was going to be a rough trip. I talked with my squad and told them to keep together. As we rocked and rolled our way across the

English Channel, our destroyers kept setting off depth charges to keep the Nazi subs at bay. There was a real risk here, as many ships had been sunk. We probably would have been really worried if we had known that just the day before, a troopship had been sunk on the very route. That fact was kept from us.

Late afternoon, I was feeling pretty tired, not to mention hungry. We had been up most of the night on the dock. I looked around and found an unoccupied bench along the bulkhead. I lay down and tried to get some shut-eye. Just as I started to drift off, when I was in that "in-between zone," a huge explosion threw me off the bench to the floor.

Chapter 5

Torpedoed

I was in a daze, and my ears were ringing. I was disoriented, and all lights had gone out. I could hear lots of yelling and some screaming. It was pitch-black. I got to my feet, holding on to the wall, and worked my way toward where I thought the rest of my squad was. After calling out a few times, I managed to locate all fifteen of them and grouped them together. Knowing the ship had been hit, I thought it best if we were on the main deck, up three levels.

The smoke was building, and men were shouting everywhere. In the black we made our way to the ladder. With the movement of the ship from the heavy seas and still in the dark, it was difficult to keep our balance, and we fell often. Without sight, it was even hard to tell which was up. We worked our way up the ladder, then to the next. Others were trying to get out as well, and it was getting hard to breathe with all the smoke. Finally, we made it to the upper deck and we could see a bit. The top deck lights and the PA

The Troop ship Leopoldville before the Torpedo

were still working. Men were everywhere, many wounded, and I could hear their cries. The dead were laid out on the deck.

We found out that we had been hit by a German torpedo, all right. The captain of the troopship came on the PA and announced we were hit but not sinking, not to panic. I got my guys together and we were all accounted for. We weren't sure at that point what to do, so we just stood by. Then I heard the strangest thing. Some of the men on deck broke out in song. They were singing Christmas carols. I guess someone thought it might ease the situation. The motion of the ship was starting to feel odd to me, but the captain came on again to reassure everyone, "All was fine." The seas were heavy. Soon the ship was listing, and the motion in the heavy seas didn't feel right to me. Not right at all.

Some of the men tried to launch the lifeboats, but in the dark and with all the confusion, it was difficult to figure out what to do. There were no crew members around to help us. Some soldiers even hacked at the ropes to free the boats, but to no avail. We found out later the Belgian crew had already launched a lifeboat, and all of them abandoned ship and us. It was the only lifeboat launched that dark night.

They had brought a British destroyer, the *Brilliant*, alongside, and it was banging and scraping against the *Leopoldville*. From my experience, I could tell the ship had a real problem and could well be sinking. I got my men together and told them I didn't think the captain was right and related my thoughts about the ship sinking. My experience working on the tug and being on the water a lot was telling me it was in fact sinking. I had made the decision to abandon ship, and with the smaller destroyer alongside, it was best if we somehow got aboard her. I told them it was not an order, but I was going to try and I thought they should come along. Only four made the decision to go. The other eleven stayed behind, going on what the captain was saying. At this point, I wasn't really scared; I just felt we needed to take action, and so we did.

I led the four men from my squad down the ladder into the dark. The *Brilliant* was much smaller. I figured we would need to go down three or four levels to get low enough to jump to the other ship. We made our way down, often waiting for men coming up. At three levels down, we moved to the side of the ship and gathered along the rail. We were low enough, but the *Brilliant* was rising and falling eight to twelve feet in the heavy seas. It was also banging and scraping against the *Leopoldville*, then pulling away about the same eight to twelve feet.

I looked down into the dark and turbulent sea between the two ships. It was a terrifying sight. Among the debris were several men who tried to make the jump and failed. Some had been crushed and were just floating; others were screaming for help. In that moment, I questioned whether this was the right thing to do, but our options were only two, stay on the sinking ship or make the jump.

Carefully I climbed over the rail and stood on the edge of the deck, holding on to the rail behind me for dear life as we rose and fell above the frothing sea below. I watched the rhythm of the ships rising and falling, banging and pulling apart. Men were yelling and calling, but I concentrated. I waited, timing my jump so as not to fall into the sea and be one of those crushed by the two ships. As the *Brilliant* rose, I timed the highest point and jumped as hard as I could. Including the distance out and down, the jump must have been twenty feet. I hit the railing of the *Brilliant* just below the waist and fell over onto the deck. I don't know if it was all the basketball or the Lord pushing me, but I made it. Sailors came running over and helped me to my feet and guided me to an area with many other solders rescued from the *Leopoldville*.

My other squad members made the jump and survived as well. It wasn't long until the sailors from the *Brilliant* realized all the banging and rubbing on the larger ship had torn a hole in her side. They were forced to untie and pull away. They couldn't pick up any more men; they needed to head back to port before we, too, sank.

I watched from the deck, and you could see the *Leopoldville* was now really listing. I could see men in the water everywhere, some swimming and flailing, some just floating facedown. I could hear cries for help, some even calling for their mothers. It wasn't but twenty minutes until the ship rolled, the bow pointed up into the air, and it went straight down. It was awful. I could see many soldiers gathered on the bow as it went down with a thousand men on board. A loud hiss came from the ship as the air was forced from her bowels as she went under. The men were compelled to jump into the stormy, cold sea. The last I saw of her was the bow covered with men hanging on and scrambling to stay out of the water; then she was gone. It was an awful sight. In the end, we had been only five miles from France.

I never again saw the eleven I left behind. I often question myself, "Perhaps I should have ordered them to come with me." Though I regretted not ordering them, I couldn't be positive the ship was going down or even that my plan would work. Five hundred men died when the ship went down. Another 300 were killed as a result of the blast. The total of 802 dead was the largest loss of life as the result of a ship sinking during the war.

The sinking of the *Leopoldville* was kept secret; actually, it was hushed up. The Belgian crew had abandoned the men on the ship. The radiomen ashore were celebrating Christmas and did not properly sound the alarm. The incidents were originally covered up by the British military and glossed over by history. We, the survivors, didn't forget.

On the deck we were given blankets and some hot chocolate. We were taken to Cherbourg, France, as planned, and dropped at another staging area. The last thing I remember is being taken down into a bunker. After that, my mind is blank until I was heading to the front. I know that during those three weeks, we had to wait for replacements for the eight hundred men we lost. We also needed to replace all our clothes and weapons since they had gone down with the ship. But I don't remember a thing during that time.

The Leopoldville on the Bottom

Chapter 6

Sent to the Front

Next thing I remember after being brought to France, I was huddled in the back of a canvas-covered troop truck with twenty other guys heading for the front. It was January 24, 1945, and it was bitter cold and snowing off and on. We had our rifles, pistols, bayonets, and our mortar batteries. The convoy was almost a mile long—trucks, artillery, medics, and supplies. It wasn't too far into the drive when we began to hear the explosions and then the gunfire of a battle in the distance. This was real, and we were here.

The Allies had moved to within miles of the German border. On December 16, 1944, fifty German divisions pushed the approaching Allied forces back into the Ardennes, creating a large bulge in the line; hence, the Battle of the Bulge. At the other side of the bulge, sixty thousand Germans were trapped along the coast. Cut off from the Reich, they received only an occasional resupply from ships that snuck through the blockade. Short of everything but ammunition, they were continuously making runs toward the German lines. The battle was on to push the

Sergent Hank Koetje in Europe

Germans back to the sea at their sub base at Lorient, France. It was here that I and the rest of the Sixty-sixth Black Panther Infantry Division were sent. Kind of fitting I would be attacking a sub base after a German sub had almost killed me.

Foxholes Dug in the Hard Ground

The front here in the west was 112 miles long, and the division was stretched thin, trying to watch the entire line and keep the Germans from pushing through. We were dropped about a quarter mile from the fighting. We walked to the lines. I was carrying an M1 as were some others in the squad. The rest were carrying the mortars and a supply of ammunition. As we approached the small town, gunfire broke out, and we had to run for cover into a nearby farmhouse and return fire. For the next two weeks, we fought with the Germans and were able to push them farther toward Lorient.

Finally, we reached an area where we could hold the German line, and it was here we would stay for the duration. We set up camp just behind the front line in a field near a hedgerow on a small family farm. We arrived late afternoon, and that night was spent digging foxholes. Lots of

Setting up and Firing the Mortar

incoming mortar and artillery rounds were exploding near us, a good incentive to dig a deep hole. At daylight, we set up our 60 mm mortar batteries; we had two of them. They are fairly short-range, and that kept us close in to the line of fighting. We would get orders to fire on certain quadrants, and we could hit them. There were even times when the fighting was so intense and close in that we were asked to fire almost on top of our own men. As sergeant, I was in charge of placing and firing the mortars.

The small farm where we were dug in was a simple place, but it did have a well where we could get water. The family, a couple on their forties and two kids, had stayed there through the fighting. There were some fruit trees, a few chickens, but not much else. We offered them C rations from time to time, but we didn't have much either.

On Patrol in the Snow.

Looking across the field from the line, we could actually see the Germans moving around. On a quiet evening, we could hear them singing "Lili Marleen." Every now and then, they would push forward, and we would come under fire. That wasn't too bad, except for the mortar-man. To drop the mortar in the tube, he had to partially stand. Once we were even forced to pull back for a time. After some fighting, we took it back and settled in our old foxholes. At night we had to be very vigilant. It was set up so that we had two hours on and two hours off all frigid night. This was our life for the next ninety-five days until the Battle of the Bulge and the war ended.

It was a bitterly cold winter, and all we had was what they called a mummy bag, better known as a fart sack. We actually welcomed the new snow; it cushioned the hard ground. Our bag was just a canvas sack large enough to hold a man. No insulation, no cushion. We slept on the cold, hard ground day after day, after day. We did get to bathe. Every ten days or two weeks, they would bring around a portable shower. We had three minutes to strip down in the below-freezing air and bathe in the lukewarm water. We almost never got our clothes washed.

We ate C rations almost all the time, but in spring we managed to find an apple or two. We even managed to catch a couple of chickens. For a real treat, we went into the nearby village where, once in a while, we could get hot bread. Wow! That was good! But day in and day out, it was food out of a can.

Chow Line

Every now and then, the Army would bring some "hot" chow out to us in the field. It was so cold, and it took so long to reach us it was never hot, but it was good.

The village where we got the bread was mostly shut down, and the people evacuated. Fortunately for us, the bakery was one of the few remaining places open.

We had a real assortment of characters in the mortar squad. There was D'Lature, from Seattle, Walker, from Illinois, who was a real joker. And a guy we called Alabama. You could not get him excited; he was slow and cool. Ultimately, Alabama was a little too slow. In the heat of battle, he dropped a mortar into the tube and failed to remove his hand quickly enough. The mortar removed most of his hand, and he was sent home. We all got along, but in those times, it was better not to make good friends. One never knew when your friend might not be there anymore. All it took was one artillery round, and they were gone.

Mail call was about every ten days. My family wrote me regularly, and it was a great comfort to hear from them. I got another letter too, a Dear John. The girl I had met from Mt. Vernon just before I left was calling it quits. She found someone closer to home. I wasn't too upset; we hadn't known each other that long. Besides, there were many guys that this happened to, some with wives and kids; and there was nothing they could do. They just had to keep on fighting.

I noticed a peculiar thing about this time. I no longer had the symptoms of asthma. The weather was wet and cold, and it should be flaring up, but I had not had an attack since I left the United States. It never did bother me again.

We had what they called reconnaissance patrols. Six men would get sent out into the area between the lines. I was selected to go on several of these recon patrols. But what they really were was a way to determine enemy location. We would approach the line until we were fired upon. When our guys saw the shooting, they could fire back at that spot. I felt more like a decoy than a recon mission. As the firing broke out, we really had to lie low so as not to get caught in the cross fire. Bullets whizzed just overhead.

Standing Watch

Artillery shells were going off almost continuously, a thousand a day in February. The Germans fired back, though not as many. We had virtually no air support at the time. Shells came into our position, and we'd run for cover and dive into our foxholes. They fired 88 mm shells at us, and they came faster than the speed of sound. We couldn't hear them unless they went overhead. Thus the saying "You never hear the one that gets you." They also had a battery of huge 340 mm guns that could lob seven-hundred-pound shells twenty-one miles. We took shells on our position on several occasions. One night, a shell hit right next to our foxhole. One of my men was killed, and two were injured. I was even nicked with a piece of shrapnel. It was just a scratch, and I never told anyone, so I didn't get a Purple Heart. With the seriously wounded around me, men with no arms or legs, I never really felt deserving of a Purple Heart anyway.

During this time, I always carried a small Bible in my pocket and read Psalms when I had a chance. When I was hunkered down in my foxhole, holding my helmet on tight with both hands, explosions going off all around me, I would repeat Psalm 23: "Though I walk through the valley of the shadow of death, I will fear no evil for Thou art with me." He was with me.

We took turns standing guard duty. The Germans had come so close we kept our bayonets on at all times. When it was pitch-black, we could see very little, and what we could see seemed to move. There were two occasions when I did see Germans moving near the lines, but I did not fire. We had wire strung around our position with hand grenades hanging from them; this told us when they were too close. When one of these went off, as they often did, it got your attention.

Finally, after continuous fighting since our arrival and 133 days of continuous fighting in the Battle of the Bulge, we were told the war was to end. There wasn't much cheering, just a real sense of relief. Word came down twenty-four hours before, but we were told to keep fighting, and bitter fighting did continue. Then the next day, it just stopped. It was quiet for the first time in months—a strange sensation. The Germans came out of their fortifications, and we could see them walking about, even waving at us.

Total casualties for the Sixty-sixth Infantry Division including the sinking of the *Leopoldville* were 78 officers and 2,171 enlisted men killed.

I received the Bronze Star for my service in this action and for the actions of my mortar squad. I am very proud to have received this award, but I keep thinking of the guys who never came home, especially those from the *Leopoldville* who never even got a chance to fight. It doesn't seem like such a long time ago.

Chapter 7

After the Fighting

The war officially ended at 11:00 a.m., just as it was supposed to. The Germans came forward into no-man's-land, and we got our first real look at the enemy we had been fighting all these months. They laid down their arms and put their hands in the air. They had surrendered to us. We came to find out that they knew how prisoners of the Russians were being treated, and they were very happy it was us who took them. They left their weapons in big piles. I pulled an infantry rifle and a .25-caliber pistol from the pile and managed to get them home, one of my few war souvenirs.

We searched their lines and rounded up all the prisoners together and took them to a staging area. I was no longer a mortar-man; we were all on guard duty. We marched the prisoners to the train station, where we boarded a train bound for Hallein, Austria. A POW camp had been constructed there, and they were ready to take our prisoners. After getting the prisoners installed in the camp, we were informed we were now prison guards. I thought the war was over and we were going home, but a lot of details needed to be tied up first. Details like war atrocities, new political systems, rebuilding infrastructure, etc. Big details. Home was looking farther away.

Since I didn't really hold any resentment to the Nazi soldiers we had as prisoners, the pressure was off and we could more or less relax around them. I had conversations with many of them, even got to know a few. One outgoing guy and I talked a lot. He was as happy as I was the war was over, and his hope was to go back to his family and the pharmacy business he was forced to leave. As it turned out, he was also a talented artist. Using a ballpoint pen, he drew a flower on my canteen cover. As he drew, he told me the story of the edelweiss flower and how rare and important it was in the German culture. As it turned out, most of our enemy, the soldiers anyway, were just guys like us doing their job. I still have the canteen cover.

Another prisoner managed to get his hands on pieces of sheet metal of different materials. Then using just a hammer, he fashioned them into great-looking platters. For these, he would trade for almost anything, but mostly for cigarettes. Since I didn't smoke and was issued a carton a week, I had lots to trade with. I got a couple of platters and some other small things. Guard duty lasted for six months until I was reassigned to occupation duty in Austria.

A train took us to Salzburg through the Alps and through some of the bombed-out cities, the beauty and the ugly. The mountains reminded me of the Cascades back home. I was anxious to get back home, but some of these men had not been home four years. This knowledge helped me; it was my turn, and I did not complain.

In Salzburg I was put in charge of the library. We were to see the library wasn't looted and eventually even got things so in order that people could check out books again. It was good duty, and we were treated very well. The Army issued us smokes and liquor, all the liquor we wanted. Good thing I was sent home after only six months of this arduous duty. While there, I got to visit some of the local sites, got to a couple of nightclubs, where we could meet and dance with local girls, and I even saw the famous puppet show they put on.

Finally, in April of 1946, it was my time to go home; it was over. It had been two years since I had seen my family, and I was excited to go. We traveled to the French coast where I boarded a ship bound for New York, along with eight thousand other returning vets. The trip was relaxing, and the men were in a jovial mood, singing and joking. I stood on the deck as we sailed past the Statue of Liberty. Some men cheered and some just stood there. It was a very emotional time; we were home, and we had survived the war. I have to tell you, though, the men who were not coming home, the men from the ship *Leopoldville* and those killed in action were also on my mind. Passing that statue was a very emotional time. She was the lady we had been fighting for.

By this time, many men had come home from the war, and there were no longer any celebrations or parades. We were simply taken to Grand Central station and put on a train to Fort Lewis.

The trip took five days, but I was so anxious it seemed like forever. My dad and uncle were waiting at the station at Fort Lewis when we arrived. Boy, it was good to see them. My big tough dad even had tears in his eyes.

We were discharged in mass the next day, and I was no longer in the Army. It seemed strange to me after all this time, four years, to be out. We were each given a four-hundred-dollar bonus for our efforts. A lot of money back then. It was a great drive home, seeing all the familiar sites around me again—the mountains, the ferry ride, and the island in the distance. Anticipation was building; I was really anxious to see my mom. I missed her very much. My father told me she had grieved for me each and every day I was at the front.

As soon as we pulled up to the house, my wonderful mother came running out, the screen door slamming behind her. With arms wide open, she took hold of me and squeezed, holding me tight. Gosh, that felt good. When we separated, I noticed Mom didn't look the same. Her face was drawn and pale; she had lost weight. Later I found she was ill with tubercular meningitis. I had only six months more with her and she was gone. I was so glad I had gotten to see her, but having her gone was difficult. She had always been there for me, encouraging me and supporting me.

Hank receiving his Bronze star from the base Commander NAS Whidbey and Representative Rick Larson.

My family had not heard about the sinking of the *Leopoldville* or the eight hundred who died. The sinking was hushed up by Britain and the United States because of all the mistakes and incompetence. They were shocked to find out this had happened, and they were not told. I didn't tell them of much else; I really wanted it in my past.

Chapter 8

The Rest of the Story

I went back to the University of Washington for a while, but I was older than most the other students and anxious to get on with my life. Neil Koetje offered me a position in his real estate company, so I began my working career in 1948. After learning the ropes, I started my own insurance company, the Henry Koetje Insurance Agency. That was sixty years ago, and I still go to work every day, but what I really enjoy are all the friends I have made over the years.

Two years after returning from the war, I married a local Dutch girl, Evelyn Dykstra, a nursing student from Everett. I became the proud parent of a daughter, Gail, and a son, Gary. Later I adopted another son, Mike. For years I thought the war was the worst experience a man could ever endure. I revised my thinking when I lost my ten-year-old son Gary to leukemia. Those were the most difficult days. On the brighter side, my daughter Gail has a beautiful voice and went on to give concerts throughout the Pacific Northwest. Currently, she is singing with the Seattle Opera. My son Mike works with UPS and is doing well.

Shortly after the war ended, I met up with my friend Gene Dunlap, the one who had given me the tug job. I had the good fortune of being introduced to his son-in-law Jack Henriot, of Burlington. Jack had only one leg, and when I asked about it, he told me he had been in the Battle of the Bulge and lost it when he stepped on a mine. We talked further, and I found he had been on the *Leopoldville* with me that night when she went down. Talk about a small world. Jack and I had experienced something few others ever have too, and we understood each other. We became great friends and still get together often to talk old times.

In 1957, some partners and I started Island Savings and Loan, later to become Interwest Bank. After opening several branch offices, we became a large company, eventually with fifty-six branches in Washington and Oregon. It was recently sold to Wells Fargo. I stayed on as a board member for forty-two years. In 1959, my brother Al joined me in the business, and later we became Koetje Insurance and Real Estate, the Koetje Agency, Inc. Then in 1962, some partners and I started Island Title Co. I was chairman of the board for several years. We expanded to ten branches before we sold the business to Chicago Title in 2000.

Hank and his wife Marilyn

I got remarried in 1987 to Marilyn Korthuis Kincaid; and between the two of us we have five children, twelve grandchildren, and six great-grandchildren. Marilyn has been a great source of support and comfort for me, and I cannot imagine a better person to spend my life with. I am a lucky man.

My hometown, Oak Harbor, honored me and my service to country in 1998 by making me the grand marshal of the Fourth of July parade. I rode the main street in a red convertible. American flags waved in the wind, a couple of fighter jets thundered overhead, and the people along the street applauded as I passed—some even saluted me. A proud moment in my life!

In 1989, I made a trip back to France and the farm where I was stationed during the war. It was much prettier than I remembered. The daughter of the family was still living on the farm and remembered when we had been there. As I stood

Hank and Marilyn the Grand Marshal 4th of July Parade

in the field along the hedgerow, sun shining, it was difficult to believe this is where I was sleeping—in a hole dug in the frozen ground, waiting for an artillery shell. It brought back many distant memories.

On this same trip to France, the French Navy took about thirty of us "*Leopoldville* survivors" out to the site where the ship had gone down. It was there, five miles off the coast from Cherbourg, that we stopped above the grave of the ship. We threw a wreath and some flowers into the sea in honor and remembrance of the 802 men who died that night on Christmas Eve 1944. Our beloved chaplain Olson offered a prayer. Though it had been forty-five years, the memories of that night came flooding back. It was, for me, a very moving moment. It brought back memories of the men I never saw again.

We also made a side trip to visit the Omaha Beach Cemetery, where ten thousand white crosses are implanted in the grass, one for each of the men who gave their lives because their country asked them to. We saw the "Walls of the Missing," where one thousand names of the dead are engraved. Many of them were from the Sixty-sixth. Some of them I recognized. I'm not ashamed to admit I shed many tears that day.

So as I hope you can see from this writing, I have had a rich and full life. I got to live in one of the most beautiful spots on the planet. I had the privilege to serve my country; I built a business and raised my wonderful children. I have a wonderful wife; I am a fortunate man. I did live the American Dream.

**Hank Koetje, 2008 at the age of 84
Still living the dream.**

Report on the *Leopoldville* Disaster (written by others)

Two days before Christmas '44 some two thousand paratroopers boarded the Belgian troopship Leopoldville at Pier 38, Southampton. Shortly thereafter, they were told to disembark. Someone had made a mistake and they were told they were on the wrong ship. Little did they know at the time how 'lucky' they had been.

In the early hours of the next day, December 24th, 2,235 men of the United States Army's 66th Infantry Division (the Black Panthers) began boarding the Leopoldville as reinforcements to fight in a fierce struggle that would become known as the Battle of the Bulge. The rest of the Division were loaded aboard the Cheshire, a British transport. In keeping with the foul-up of the previous day, none were assigned specific quarters and they were berthed wherever there was room as they boarded and not, by unit, squad or company. Confusion seemed to be the order of the day. No lifeboat drill was performed and the life belts were secured in their stowage compartments. None were issued to the men onboard. The Leopoldville was protected by escort ships, including the British Destroyer Brilliant, but no air cover was made available even though the threat of attack by German subMarines was high.

It was to be a short voyage across the Channel. To date, the Leopoldville had already carried nearly 125,000 soldiers to various destinations without trouble and, because of there being so many Allied warships in the Channel, no one seemed too worried about the possibility of submarine attacks. Yet, the troopships were escorted by four destroyers.

Around 2 PM, the Captain of the Leopoldville received the order to begin a zigzag course. A first submarine alert sounded thirty minutes later then a second one. By then, the sea was running eight to nine feet. By 4 PM, the sea had reached a state of Force 6 and the Leopoldville was but 25 miles from their point of destination, the port of Cherbourg.

By 6 PM, the Leopoldville was five miles from Cherbourg. Some fifteen minutes earlier, Oberleutnant Gerhard Meyer, Captain of the Type VII C-class submarine U-486 had begun tracking the Leopoldville in its sight. Two torpedoes were launched at 5:56 PM and one reached its mark at precisely 6 PM.

From that moment on, it was bedlam. What took place is amply described in detail in several books but suffice to say that men onboard the Leopoldville received little, if any, help nor directions from the crew. The Captain of the Leopoldville, Captain Limbor, did nothing! No distress message, no call for assistance, nothing. According to many survivors, the Belgian crew abandoned the sinking ship and left the American soldiers to fend for themselves. The British Commander in charge of the convoy ordered the Leopoldville's anchor dropped to prevent the troopship from drifting into a minefield outside the harbor. While this solved one problem, it created another. When a tug arrived on the scene, the dropped anchor prevented it from towing the sinking vessel into shore. Murphy's law states that whatever can go wrong will. On Christmas Eve 1944, Murphy's law was in full effect. Delayed radio transmissions for help, delayed response of rescue craft, heavy seas and freezing temperatures were just a few of the many things that sealed the soldiers fates. And it being Christmas Eve, serviceman at an American base in Cherbourg who could have aided the stricken Leopoldville were taking a night off from the war, either partying or attending church. No one seemed to be around to help.

Officers onboard the other troopship in the convoy, the Cheshire thought they had heard a muffled explosion and actually saw the debacle onboard the Leopoldville but, there having been no radio traffic calling for assistance, they were left in the dark as to what was actually taking place. Most of those taking to the lifeboats from the Leopoldville were members of the crew.

All this time, those ashore who could have been of some help in the rescue were celebrating Christmas Eve or were away on leave. No one in Cherbourg knew there was any problem only five miles offshore. So it came as a complete surprise when the port authorities received a radio message from the Convoy Commander, Captain John Pringle of H.M.S. Brilliant informing them they were taking on survivors and requesting assistance! It was the first news of trouble afoot received by Cherbourg's personnel.

By the time the rescue effort began to be coordinated at Cherbourg, the men onboard the Leopoldville still had not been told the ship was fast sinking under them. The Brilliant effected a daring rescue and by 7:30 PM had succeeded in getting nearly 700 survivors. Oddly enough, the other three destroyer escorts headed for harbor after their futile attempt to sink the U-boat. They had heard no call for assistance from the Leopoldville

Fearing for the safety of his ship which by then had been much bandied about while rescuing the men from the Leopoldville, the Brilliant disengaged and made for Cherbourg. The Leopoldville sank beneath the waves at 8:30 PM. More men were saved by the rescue boats which by then had made it to the scene from Cherbourg. Only one officer, the Captain, from the Leopoldville lost his life. By the end of that terrible night, 802* American soldiers were dead, many drowning or freezing to death in the icy waters of the English Channel. These soldiers represented youths from 47 of the then 48 United States. New York State alone lost 80 young men, including 39 from New York City. Many of those killed were only 18 to 21 years old and 493 of the bodies were never recovered. Three sets of brothers were killed, including two sets of twins.

Because of wartime censorship and to cover-up the mistakes made by the various governments and officials involved, the disaster was not reported to the news media. Survivors were told by the British and American governments to keep quiet. Amazingly, relatives of the victims received notices that their loved ones were Missing in Action, even though the U.S. War Department knew them all to have perished. Later, the men were declared Killed in Action, but even then no details of their deaths were divulged to their families. After the war, the tragedy was considered an embarrassment to the Allies and all reports were filed away as secret by the American and British governments. Families of victims searched vainly for information about the deaths of their loved ones. Only in 1996—over 50 years later—did the British declassify documents relating to the sinking of the Leopoldville.

The Leopoldville disaster was the worst tragedy to ever befall an American Infantry Division as the result of an enemy submarine attack. Yet, this is more than a story about a terrible wartime tragedy, it is about how governments, in order to hide their own mistakes, can hide the truth from those who need it the most.

Footnote:

The U-486 submarine that sunk the *Leopoldville* was itself sunk on April 12, 1945, in the North Sea northwest of Bergen, Norway, by torpedoes from the British submarine HMS *Tapir*. All forty-eight crew onboard were lost.

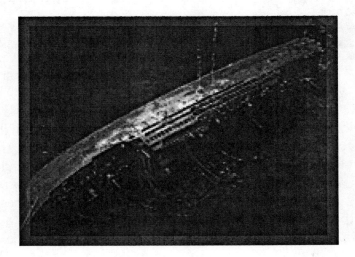

Adolph Paul "Mickey" Meisch Sr.

Eagles Fly in PBYs

"That's the girl I'm going to marry! I said to myself," with the same alert twinkle and love in his eyes.

He told me, "I knew she was the one the minute I saw her."

Although Adolph was a young man with a small build, he must have made up for it with his daring showmanship and athletic prowess. He swept her off her skates and into his arms. Adolph is an eagle in every sense of the word. He met his mate, Dolores, at the skating rink in Anacortes, Washington, the first time he was stationed at NAS Whidbey.

To date, they have been married sixty-three years, have nine children, eighteen grandchildren, and fifteen great-grandchildren. Adolph, or "Mickey" as Dolores calls him; both still have the glow of newlyweds after all these years when they look at each other. Dolores and Adolph's home is surrounded with family pictures, portraits of generations of Meisch eagles. They are a testament to Adolph's pride in his Luxembourg German heritage. His great-grandfather, John Gengler, brought his family to Caledonia, Minnesota, in the 1880s. Adolph's grandfather John Meisch was a "gendarme" in Luxemburg. Adolph was a patriotic young eagle with a natural instinct for flying.

"At the age of seventeen, I went to Civil Aviation Ground School while completing high school. I enlisted in the Navy on November 22, 1943, at Aurora, Illinois. Then I was sent to the Great Lakes on December 2 for boot camp. In February 1944, I continued my aviation training in engine mechanics and the ordinances divisions at NAS Memphis, Tennessee. By August 1944, I was in the Naval Free Gunnery School at Yellow Water, Florida. At NAS Jacksonville, Florida, I had combat aircrew training on the consolidated PBYs.

"Prior to May 12, 1945, I was sent to NAS San Diego, California, for further assignment to Whidbey Island. It had taken nearly a year, but I was going to war in the Pacific! Assuming Whidbey Island was somewhere in the South Pacific. However, I was extremely confused when they put me on a train heading north. Four days by train doesn't get you to the South Pacific. NAS Whidbey Island, Washington, would be my good fortune, a seaplane base with PBYs.

"The PBYs are slow-moving (135 mph) vulnerable planes, yet they were capable of sinking tons of enemy warships to the bottom of the Pacific. Just as proficiently, these planes were used to rescue Australian and American Navy crewmen from the waters of the South Pacific during the war.

"I was extremely disappointed that I was not sent to the South Pacific because I wanted to be in on the action for which I had been trained. But as luck or misfortune, I saw the war from different Pacific temperate zones."

The war with Japan along the Aleutian chain is often referred to as the "Forgotten War." But the military personnel stationed there to protect the Canadian and U.S. coastlines from invasion by the Japanese remember it. Japan had already occupied two of the Aleutian Islands. Japanese submarines had been spotted in the Pacific Ocean waters during the war. Hollywood celebrities braving subzero weather and dangerous flying conditions to entertain the troops knew the war on the remote northern edge of the Pacific Rim was for real.

"Other pilots and crews flew in supplies or ferried lend-lease aircraft from Great Falls, Montana, to Fairbanks, Alaska. The Russians had no trouble flying those lend-lease planes over our boundaries from Fairbanks to Russia. At the time, Russia played Germany against the United States. The Russians didn't come into the war on our side until it was obvious that we were going to win. Remember, if we had come down on their side of the border, they would have confiscated the plane from our crew. We flew the chain of the Aleutians, establishing and supplying more Navy bases. Flying our PBYs out of NAS Whidbey, we were patrolling for Japanese submarines. We never saw one, but it was our job to keep vigilant all the time from eight to sixteen hours, looking for the Japanese in the oceans and coastlines. We did rescue a pilot of an F6F plane. That was the only rescue we made, and that was well after the war was over.

"After Dolores and I were married on January 26, 1946, our first temporary home was a Quonset hut near the Victory homes on Regatta in Oak Harbor. Each Quonset hut had two two-bedroom apartments, one at each end."

We lived there two months before we moved to Anacortes. By this time Adolph and I were expecting our first child," said Dolores.

"Like most military personnel, I hated being away from my wife. But I loved the Navy and my PBYs. I find it easy to remember one such flight from Adak to Nome. The weather conditions on the mainland had made it impossible to deliver the Christmas mail up to Nome until January 26, 1946. We flew into Cold Bay from NAS Whidbey in horrible weather that other planes couldn't handle. In fact, the weather could be blamed for nearly 95 percent of the planes that went down and men killed.

"We flew PBYs, also called Catalinas. It's not a nice airplane to fly. It's not nice to work on, there's nothing slower flying, and hundreds were shot down. It's still my favorite plane. During the last year of the war with Japan, they only shot down a few of our planes. It was the weather that brought down more planes out of the sky, and sunk more of our naval ships.

"We flew the mailbags out to Adak in the PBY. I moved into another Quonset hut with my flight crew. We flew the mail from Adak to Nome then on up to the Pribilof Islands. We dropped the mail off, literally. We flew over the St. George and St. Paul islands, past them to the Little Diomede Island in the middle of the Bering Strait. It's located just one kilometer from the International Date Line and only four kilometers from the Russian island of Big Diomede. We dropped mail off to the Little Diomede. If we had crossed the International Date Line even accidentally, our plane could have been shot down by the Russians. As it was, they escorted us with fighter planes away from Big Diomede, back to Little Diomede and back to Nome.

"I remember another little incident when we dropped the mail off to one of the little islands of St. George or St. Paul. The mailbag, duffel bag, hit on their radio building and the bag tore wide open and the mail was being blown in all directions. As soon as the mail was airborne again, the men came out of the buildings running after the letters in the wind.

"I flew 'shot gun' when we delivered supplies and goods from Adak and Nome. I had a Quonset hut in Nome when I wasn't flying. There's also an island called Sand Point in the Aleutians. There was a story going around that one of our pilots had to make an emergency landing on the island and one native women chased after him and wouldn't let him leave.

"The williwaw, a sideways horizontal-like tornado wind, would strike without warning. Once we flew through a williwaw, an extremely severe turbulent wind, when we were coming in for a landing at Adak. It twisted the plane over and upright again before we even knew we had been hit. Oh, we knew what we had been hit with, but we had no time to be scared. In fact, when we were flying, we had to concentrate on keeping in the sky, so there was no time to succumb to fear. A williwaw can happen at any time, any season, or day because of the strong winds that never stop in the Aleutians.

"One time we took off from Kodiak in a PBY, cruising at ten thousand feet. The wind was so strong that we were not going to get to Adak that day. The plane only travels 100-115 knots, and in a

100-knot wind, you're not going anywhere. We ended up staying at Kodiak for three days, just waiting for the wind to die down. These winds of 100 knots or more could last as long as three solid days. I remember two Army guys wanted to go to the club in the wind. I don't know why they even thought about it because everything was closed. They were killed trying to walk from their barracks to the club because they got lost in the blowing wind and snow.

"Another story happened when we were in Nome. We were taking off when the oil cooler blew. In the time it took us to blow the oil cooler, we pumped out forty-two gallons of oil in thirty-five-degrees-below-zero weather. That oil sprayed on the side of the plane, turned to tar in the time it took to circle the airfield. After we got the plane back in the hangar, it took two and a half hours for that tar to get warm enough to start dripping on the floor.

[This is a copy of a photo in the author's husband's airplane scrapbook.]

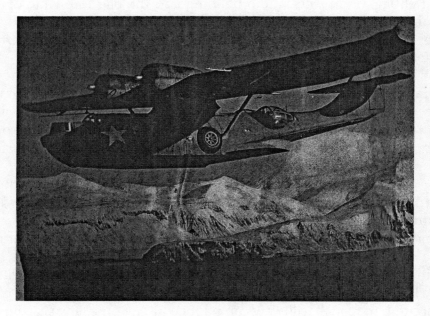

"The second time that I was on a three-month assignment in the Aleutians, I flew the PB4Y-2, Privateer. I arrived in the summer of 1947, and the williwaws were still there to greet me. When this assignment was finished, I came home to Dolores and the baby and finished my four-year enlistment.

Addendum

"I re-enlisted at NAS Whidbey and went on inactive duty. After moving the family to NAS Glenview in Illinois, I returned to active duty. I served as a trainer for the Navy reservists for nearly fifteen years. During the Korean Conflict, I trained the reservists who went into war once again in the South Pacific. Had I been asked by the Navy to serve in the Korean Conflict, I would have gone. However, the Navy apparently needed me as a trainer: teaching freshmen pilot and crew how to maintain the Navy's version of the DC-3 and DC-4 transporters of troops and supplies.

"On January 22, 1957, I was returning from California after picking up the body of a military pilot who had been killed in a midair collision over Albuquerque, New Mexico. On the return flight in our DC-4, the weather conditions were too treacherous at NAS Glenview for us to land. We decided to fly on to a civilian airport in Ypsilanti, Michigan. On the approach in a blinding blizzard, the altimeter registered an eight-hundred-feet level. However, the instrument was frozen at that reading. Abruptly we found ourselves at ground level, and the copilot reported that we had hit the deck. The DC-4 had descended into a frozen gravel pit near a local farmer's house. The farmer rushed out of his house to watch the plane plow and skate around until it crashed into an embankment around the perimeter of the crash-landing site.

"On impact, both wings were ripped off and the plane spewed burning fuel across the ice. The fuselage skidded and bounced out of the inferno another six hundred feet before it went into a sliding halt. I was positioned between the two pilots, exactly where I was expected to be for a normal landing. The pilot sustained a fractured leg and the copilot was killed. I sustained three crushed and shattered bones in my left leg, a broken jaw, multiple cuts, abrasions, and a brain concussion."

According to the surgeon, to still be alive after that, Adolph was "one tough ol' bird." We recognize them as eagles here in the Northwest. Adolph spent a whole year in recovery and rehabilitation before he could return to his duties as a trainer.

During 1963, the threat of Communism in Cuba was on every American's mind. President John F. Kennedy was dealing with the "Bay of Pigs," and Adolph was dealing with the intense drama by training more Navy support personnel in the advent of WWIII.

In 1965, Adolph was transferred back to NAS Sand Point, Washington. He had become a naval flight engineer. They lived in Bothell, where Dolores was well qualified to run a day care in their home.

"After retirement in 1967, I had a new job 'in a wonderful place to work' for which I was well trained: Kenmore Air Harbor. I was an FAA-certified inspector while there. As a licensed civilian commercial pilot, I had flown many different aircraft, but the PBY remained my favorite. I worked there for the next twenty years before moving back to Whidbey Island.

"On Whidbey, I was hired as an inspector for the Navy-Whidbey Flying Club, and instrumental in creating the PBY Foundation in Oak Harbor. It has always been a family dream to see the PBY retire with honors here on NAS Whidbey Island. Please visit their website: *www.pbyma.org/gb.html* for more information regarding the PBY Memorial Fund."

It has occurred to me, after talking with several of our white-haired veterans, just how much they have in common with our nation's symbol of freedom: the majestic bald eagle.

Each generation of eagles set the standards of excellence for the generation that follows. As long as the rest of us remember to value the contributions of each generation of veterans, we will prevail as a nation of eagles.

It would be a generous gesture of gratitude to every veteran who fought in the Pacific Theater, if everyone who reads this article on Chief Adolph Paul Meisch Sr. and/or remembers their favorite veteran by sending a $10 donation to the PBY Memorial Foundation Fund, PO Box 941, Oak Harbor, Washington, 98277.

Robert "Bob" Muzzall

Family, Respect, and Responsibility

The Muzzall family moved to Whidbey Island in 1912 from Michigan. Bob believes in the family values that he was taught by his parents around the dinner table as one of six children. He learned respect for women, for each other, and taking responsibility within the family from his mother. His father taught his heirs to love nature, respect, and take responsibility for the environment.

Their family farm sits on the bluff above Penn Cove. They've watched the changes and development along the shoreline and the losses of the "blackfish" (orcas) that arrived every year until 1972. Bob imitated the sounds of the whales clearing their blowholes, which could be heard from any distance on their farm. They would drop what they were doing to go watch the pods come in the cove from their bluff.

Bob was quite an athlete at OHHS, but he was on crutches at his graduation. Bob had slipped and jammed a knot of a tree into his knee earlier while he was gathering cedar logs suitable for fence posts. That accident would change the course of Bob's life. The knee took nearly two years to heal because of the infection in the joint. The leg had to be straightened and immobilized before it would heal. Half of that time he lived and worked with his sister in Dukane, Michigan.

"I was in Dukane with my sister when Pearl Harbor was bombed. It was no surprise to my parents when two of my brothers and another sister enlisted in the military. At age twenty-one, I came home with intentions of enlisting too. With my brothers away, my dad needed me to help the rest of the family run the farm, which wasn't what I wanted to do, but I thought I should do what my father asked.

"Our family had suffered the loss of another son due to a car accident. David, a beloved son and brother, had died the night of my high school graduation. My parents did not encourage me to join up for the military. Quite the contrary, my dad and I had several arguments on the subject. My brother Murray, a student at WSU, had enlisted in the Army infantry as a private in 1941 and was sent to the Pacific for a year or two. Then the Army decided to send him to Officer's Candidate School in Australia. As it happened, we had relatives there, so he had a pleasant time visiting them before going back to the Pacific.

"Another two years passed, and I tried once again to enlist in the Army Air Corps. During the physical for the Army Aviation Cadets, it took a note from Dr. Carskadden stating that the knee was stable. Finally, the Army decided I had potential and sent me off to Oklahoma for basic training. I started my military service by going to flight training and learning to fly. Sometime during the middle of basic training, the Army decided they didn't need me as a pilot. So I was sent to flight ground school, navigation, and radio school.

"While I was in Oklahoma for basic training, I made friends with a couple there. They proceeded to do a little matchmaking with a friend they knew back home in Madison, Wisconsin. Evelyn and I had a long distance, yet short, courtship, courtesy of the U.S. mail. Evee was a student at the University in Madison. Ironically, I had been sent there for radio training in Madison, Wisconsin. After all those daily letters to my sweetheart, I finally met Evelyn and her family in Wisconsin. In advanced radio school, I was trained for and used a new system for locating lost and/or missing planes. If the navigator was wounded or lost, the crew contacted me by radio and I helped them get their bearings. It didn't matter that I was competent, mature, well trained. I was still waiting for overseas replacement orders.

When I completed my training, with some fast-talking, Evelyn and I convinced her family that Evee (Evelyn) should come on the train with me. Evee immediately filled that void in my heart left with the death of my older brother, Lt. Murray Muzzall. Murray had been killed in heavy fire leading a charge against the Japanese in Mindanao in the Philippines. I took the loss very personal. We were very close in spite of the difference between our ages.

"Maybe it was the long train ride, the long dark train tunnels, or the beauty of the Northwest, or that persuasive future mother-in-law, but Evee and I got married right in the living room of my family's home. We had a two-day honeymoon in Canada. That raised a few eyebrows back in Wisconsin and created blizzard conditions between

Evee and her mother. I'm sure that her mother really wanted to be a part of the wedding preparations. I had to report back to my training in Texas. So Evee and I stayed with our friends until we could get our own place.

"Things were winding down in Europe, and I was waiting on the Army. Ironically, when the war ended, I still belonged to the Army Air Corps. They didn't need radio operators, but they could use someone trained to work in the airport control tower. So they sent me back to school again, and then on to Mariana, Florida, until that base closed down. Bases were closing down all over, so I was sent to work in the control tower in Panama City, Florida, where I trained pilots how to identify enemy planes, while waiting to get out of the service.

"Finally, in 1946, I came home to my wife. The base had been located near a pulp mill, and they didn't think pregnant women should smell those fumes from the mill. Evee was miserable with morning sickness because of the fumes. Her doctors advised her to move away. So she came home to farm life on Whidbey, which was completely new to her. I saw a lot of the U.S. throughout my training, and it seemed like I had to go north in the wintertime and south in the summer. 'That's not the way to do it!' After a few years, Evee and I took on the business running of the farm and the dairy. I was proud of the way Evee took to family and island life.

"My younger brother Lyle 'Ben' Muzzall was in a tank maintenance battery and saw action in France, Germany, and the liberation of prisoner of war camps and concentration prisons. Ben came home. Our sister, Eleanor, a WAVE, in Norman, Oklahoma was now married to Chuck, from Detroit, Michigan. Eleanor won a lottery for 114 acres of farmland in California. The Army Corps of Engineers drained Tule Lake, making the land available for industrious farmers to lease land from her. This new income allowed Eleanor to be able to go back to college, while raising their five children to become a teacher. She moved to Anchorage, where she taught school and maintained the library until she retired."

"What advice would you have for young families today?"

"Appreciate the children, and show them that respect and responsibility start at home. And those discussions around the dinner table help grow relationships."

"Regrets?"

"Yes, there was a time when I wanted to go to Europe during the war. I was thoroughly disgusted with the Army Air Corps. They trained me for so many jobs, and I never got to use that training in defense of my country. Now that I'm older, I have learned that there was a reason why I never reached the shores of Europe. Apparently, the Lord had other intentions for me. Perhaps that's why my family is and has always been so important to me."

Bob passed away from pancreatic cancer shortly after our initial interview, preceding his wife by mere months. Ironically, his son, Rob used to babysit our boys when we lived in Penn Cove, and two of his three delightful granddaughters of the "Three Sisters' Cattle Co.," were in my classes at Oak Harbor Elementary, where Bob once attended high school. I think Bob would have agreed with me, the Lord works in mysterious ways.

CPSIA information can be obtained at www.ICGtesting.com
Printed in the USA
LVOW08s0349261013

358597LV00002B/153/P